Maurice Bloch has for many years been developing an original and influential theory of ritual. In this book he synthesises a radical theory of religion. Rituals in a great many societies deny the transience of life and of human institutions. Bloch argues that they enact this denial by symbolically sacrificing the participants themselves, so allowing them to participate in the immortality of a transcendent entity. Such sacrifices are achieved through acts of symbolic violence, ranging from bodily mutilations to the killing of animals. The theme is developed with reference to rituals of many types, from a variety of ethnographic sources, and Bloch shows that even exogamous marriage rituals can be reinterpreted in the light of this thesis. He concludes by considering the indirect relation of symbolic and ritual violence to political violence.

Prey into hunter

THE LEWIS HENRY MORGAN LECTURES 1984

presented at
The University of Rochester
Rochester, New York

Lewis Henry Morgan Lecture Series

Fred Eggan: *The American Indian: Perspectives for the Study of Social Change*

Ward H. Goodenough: *Description and Comparison in Cultural Anthropology*

Robert J. Smith: *Japanese Society: Tradition, Self, and the Social Order*

Sally Falk Moore: *Social Facts and Fabrications: "Customary Law" on Kilimanjaro, 1880–1980*

Nancy Munn: *The Fame of Gawa: A Symbolic Study of Value Transformation in a Mussim (Papua New Guinea) Society*

Lawrence Rosen: *The Anthropology of Justice: Law as Culture in Islamic Society*

Stanley Jeyaraja Tambiah: *Magic, Science, Religion, and the Scope of Rationality*

Prey into hunter
The politics of religious experience

MAURICE BLOCH

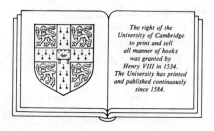

The right of the
University of Cambridge
to print and sell
all manner of books
was granted by
Henry VIII in 1534.
The University has printed
and published continuously
since 1584.

CAMBRIDGE UNIVERSITY PRESS

CAMBRIDGE

NEW YORK   PORT CHESTER

MELBOURNE   SYDNEY

Published by the Press Syndicate of the University of Cambridge
The Pitt Building, Trumpington Street, Cambridge CB2 1RP
40 West 20th Street, New York, NY 10011-4211, USA
10 Stamford Road, Oakleigh, Melbourne 3166, Australia

First published 1992

Printed in Great Britain at the University Press, Cambridge

British Library cataloguing in publication data
Bloch, Maurice
Prey into hunter: the politics of religious experience. –
(The Lewis Henry Morgan lectures)
1. Rituals
I. Title
306.4

Library of Congress cataloguing in publication data
Bloch, Maurice
Prey into hunter: the politics of religious experience / Maurice Bloch
p.   cm. – (The Lewis Henry Morgan lectures; 1987)
Includes bibliographical references and index.
ISBN 0 521 41154 8. – ISBN 0 521 42312 0 (pbk)
1. Violence – Religious aspects. 2. Sacrifice. 3. Experience
(Religion) 4. Religion and civilization. I. Title. II. Series.
BL570.B53   1992
291.3'4 – dc20   91–11357   CIP

ISBN 0 521 41154 8 hardback
ISBN 0 521 42312 0 paperback

Contents

Foreword

In 1987, Professor Bloch delivered the Lewis Henry Morgan Lectures at the University of Rochester on 17, 19, 24 and 29 February. His general title was then, as it is now, *Prey into Hunter: The Politics of Religious Experience*, with the individual lectures entitled 'Initiation: the containment of strength', 'Sacrifice: the aggressive death', 'Marriage: being swallowed and swallowing', 'Myth and millennium: the uncertainties of continuity'. Revision, expansion and rearrangement of the originals have resulted in the present version – an intriguing study that offers readers ample intellectual fare.

Unlike his earlier work on the Merina, dealt with in *From Blessing to Violence*, Professor Bloch is not here concerned with an historical examination of the examples he considers, although he pursues some of the more general ideas adumbrated in *From Blessing to Violence*. His present study is aimed at establishing 'the irreducible core of the ritual process' and the factors determining it. Part of that core is what he terms 'rebounding violence'. A major feature of this book is the elaboration of this concept, by examination of the ways in which it is manifested in a wide range of rituals.

Professor Bloch distinguishes this work from much that he has done earlier, since he is not here primarily concerned with history. He also makes clear the differences between his concepts and conclusions and those of many earlier anthropologists working on the same or closely related problems. This is a generalising comparative study, quite clearly intended to challenge much widely accepted work. The possibilities implied by Professor Bloch's present-ation are very considerable indeed, and it is obvious that he has in mind not only anthropological work, but historical work as well.

The limits of a foreword preclude discussion of Professor Bloch's complex and ingenious analysis of the widely distributed examples he has adduced to illustrate his points. It should be noted here that this version of the original lectures retains much of the liveliness and freshness of Professor Bloch's oral presentation, so the distinction between auditors and readers becomes

xi

blurred, and the book invites all to engage in the continuing construction of anthropology.

Alfred Harris
Editor
The Lewis Henry Morgan Lectures

Acknowledgements

This book is based on the four Lewis Henry Morgan lectures which were delivered at the University of Rochester. I would like to thank this university both for its invitation and for its hospitality during the period of the lectures. I was able to advance greatly the preparation of the text during a month-long visit as a guest of the Danish Centre for Research in the Humanities where I enjoyed ideal working conditions and much intellectual stimulation. I would also like to thank the National Museum of Ethnology, Senri, Japan, for having invited me in 1984 for a period of three months during which I was able to acquaint myself with the anthropology of Japan. I am particularly grateful to Tom Gibson, André Iteanu, Wazir-Jahan Karim, David Lan, Godfrey Lienhardt, Jonathan Parry and Maria Phylactou. They are anthropologists whose work I discuss in this book and who have been willing to comment on earlier drafts of the relevant sections. They do not necessarily endorse my reinterpretation of the material but their suggestions have enabled me to avoid some major ethnographic errors. I have also received help for the section on Japan from Shige Tanabe and for the section on early Christianity from Bernhard Lang. I also greatly benefited from comments of earlier drafts of part or all of this book from Jean Bloch, Fenella Cannell, Janet Carsten, Gillian Gillison, Eric Hirsch, Lisette Josephides, Fritz Kramer, Jonathan Parry, Warren Shapiro and Gabrielle Vom Bruck. Finally I want to again thank Fenella Cannell for her invaluable help in preparing this manuscript for publications.

1

Introduction

This book is a theoretical essay, an exploration of an idea which was suggested by an earlier much more specific and much less speculative piece of work. This earlier study was a history of the Malagasy circumcision ritual which was published as *From Blessing to Violence* (Bloch 1986). This historical study revealed that, while some aspects of the ritual adapted functionally to changing politico-economic circumstances, other aspects remained unchanged through time. These unchanging aspects were not in any sense arbitrary; rather they made up a central minimal structure or 'core' of the ritual process. The different historical forms taken at one time or another by Malagasy circumcision always related to this core as logical elaborations of it, although at some periods the ritual was very much elaborated while at others it was reduced to its simplest form.

Since this simplest form of the ritual process persisted unchanged even when its context was changing, it presented a problem for those theories which explain phenomena in terms of their fit with other aspects of culture and society. The explanation could only be that it depended on matters which could not be reduced to the specific, historical circumstances in which the performances of the ritual occurred. I present this essay as an exploration of the nature of this irreducible core of the ritual process, and the factors which do in fact determine it.

The enquiry is not, however, confined to Madagascar. In fact, while in one light Merina circumcision ritual appears as specific and typical of well-known Malagasy cultural themes, in another light it seems to concern aspects of the human predicament which would be relevant in very many cultures. The structure which I perceive in the basic minimal form of Merina ritual seems to me to be present in a wide range of religious phenomena from many parts of the world, each of which again displays these two sides: each belongs to its own specific culture, yet each also shows a striking structural resemblance to the others. This claim to quasi-universality may seem surprising. However, it will be justified at least in part if the suggestion I shall develop in this book

1

about the relationship between religious process and notions of biological life and death are found to be convincing.

To pursue this exploration, I have deliberately chosen an extremely varied set of ethnographic examples. All of these are forms of what I would broadly refer to as religious phenomena. But although it was Merina circumcision which started me off on this search, not all of my examples are rituals of the same sort. Thus, the Merina circumcision ritual could be described as initiation, as could the Papua New Guinean example discussed in the next chapter, but none of the other examples in the book could be called initiation rituals. And although I find the unchanging aspects of religious process mainly in rituals, the book also takes in subjects which anthropologists would not normally call rituals at all: myth from Malaysia (chapter 7) and some observations which might more usually be found labelled as kinship or politics (chapter 5). The range of rituals discussed in the book includes rituals from East Africa and South East Asia which are normally called sacrifices (chapter 3), spirit mediumship from southern Africa and the Philippines (chapters 3 and 5), millenarian cults from Madagascar and the Near East (chapter 6), marriage rituals from Tibet and ancient Rome (chapter 5) and total ritual systems from India and Japan which contain a little of all these elements (chapter 4).

This crossing of established categories is of course nothing new. Anthropologists are increasingly familiar with the idea that such terms as 'sacrifice', 'possession' and 'initiation' have a very limited validity in religious anthropology. Such definitions are always rooted in a specific cultural tradition, whether that of the author or of the people he writes about, and are therefore inadequate for cross-cultural analysis. They may be used provisionally, as convenient pointers, but if their application is stretched beyond that they become arbitrary. If general theoretical interpretations are to be attempted at all, they cannot be confined within these sorts of definitions. What is needed, and what is attempted in part here, is some much more all-embracing framework which sidesteps some of the old problems.

This is undoubtedly an exercise fraught with dangers, both methodological and theoretical. Having got hold of the idea of a widely present structure within religious processes, we would surely find it easy to make a tendentious selection of examples, and make this structure appear to be present everywhere. Or else, one might present the evidence in such a way as to highlight only the aspects which fit the theory, obscuring those which do not. Whether I have sufficiently avoided these pitfalls must in the end be judged by the reader, since it would be impossible to present enough examples to demonstrate generality at the level at which the claim is being made. The selection of examples from very different cultures may go some way towards substantiating the argument, but more importantly readers and critics may choose to continue the exercise by trying to see whether what is proposed here stands up to the test of other cases they know. As for the problem of skewed presentation, I hope at least that by taking my (inevitably much abbreviated) ethnographic examples from widely available sources I have made it easy for readers to go back to the originals and consider for themselves whether the examples fit my argument.

The theoretical problems raised by the enterprise are rather different. First, there is a familiar difficulty with arguments such as this. Inevitably, the demonstration of the presence of structural similarities in the religious phenomena discussed seems almost to beg the question; it presumes the existence of what it wants to show exists. This problem is I think to some extent unavoidable, and the argument will finally depend on its ability to persuade the independent reader that the structures discussed are real and not merely the imagination of the author. However, this is a not uncommon problem of attempts to push beyond established theoretical and ethnographic interpretations, and I hope to convince the reader that it will be worth the risk.

Secondly, there is the problem of what is meant by the concept under discussion in this book, of a minimum irreducible structure which is common to many ritual and other religious phenomena. This will become gradually clearer in its specifics as the argument is developed through the examples in the main text. I should, however, perhaps dispense with two general points here. Firstly, I do not intend to suggest something like a 'lowest common denominator' of a range of examples. This sort of definition (for instance of 'kinship' or 'marriage') characterised much anthropological writing in the fifties and sixties (Needham 1971), but the similarities claimed between cases have almost always been much too vague to be helpful.

My intentions are somewhat closer to those of writers who, like the historian of religions Mircea Eliade, explicitly claimed to be describing an essence or 'archetype' of a particular class of phenomena. Eliade claimed that in his 'archetypes' he was able to identify the irreducible components of religious ideas in different cultures (Eliade 1969). My approach is similar to Eliade's in that both his 'archetypes' and the minimal structures which I identify are seen as the product of general characteristics of human beings. Yet the general characteristics envisaged in the two arguments could not be more different. Eliade's archetypes do not in any way relate to the material existence of human beings. The character of his archetypes therefore remains vague and mystical.

By contrast with Eliade, I argue that the startling quasi-universality of the minimal religious structures I identify rests on something much more specific. That is, it derives from the fact that the vast majority of societies represent human life as occurring within a permanent framework which transcends the natural transformative process of birth, growth, reproduction, ageing and death. It is the near-universality of this construct, I argue, which accounts for the occurrence and re-occurrence of the same structural pattern in ritual and other religious representations at many times and in many places. Ultimately, therefore, I am seeking to establish a connection between a religious construction and universal human constraints. Of course, this book cannot be considered to have provided a satisfactory demonstration of such a connection, and does not claim to do so, but it was with this aim in view that the exploration of which it forms a part was undertaken, and in this direction that the theoretical conclusions presented here will lead.

The nature of the ritual processes I am concerned with will gradually become clearer in the light of the examples discussed in subsequent chapters. However, a brief presentation can be given here, as a preliminary guide to the argument which follows.

These irreducible structures of religious phenomena are ritual representations of the existence of human beings in time. In fact this ritual representation is a simple transformation of the material processes of life in plants and animals as well as humans. The transformation takes place in an idiom which has two distinguishing features: first, it is accomplished through a classic three-stage dialectical process, and secondly it involves a marked element of violence or (to use a term less familiar in our society than in many of those discussed here) of conquest. I shall refer to this process as the idiom of 'rebounding violence'.

In all cultures there is a level of perception where birth is seen as either the beginning of or at least a significant stage in the period of growth which has the potential to engender further reproduction. The reproductive stage is in turn seen at one level of perception as followed by a period of gradual decay leading to death. This process is perceived as common to all kinds of living things. Further, the transformative dialectic of different kinds of living things is seen as linked, if only because one species provides food for another.

The representation of life in rituals begins with a complete inversion of everyday understandings. The life evoked in rituals is an 'other' life, described by such words as 'beyond' and 'invisible', and located 'in the sky', 'under the earth' or 'on a mountain where nobody goes'. In these ritual representations, instead of birth and growth leading to a successful existence, it is weakening and death which lead to a successful existence. For example, initiation frequently begins with a symbolic 'killing' of the initiates, a 'killing' which negates their birth and nurturing. The social and political significance of such a passage is that by entering into a world beyond process, through the passage of reversal, one can then be part of an entity beyond process, for example, a member of a descent group. Thus, by leaving this life, it is possible to see oneself and others as part of something permanent, therefore life-transcending.

Moving out of this world into another can, however, only be a partial answer to the problem posed by the politico-social requirement of constructing a totality consisting of living beings, which is, unlike its constituent parts, permanent. The reason why the move into the beyond is ultimately politically unsatisfactory is simply that, if you leave this life, you leave this life, and so the constructed totality becomes of no relevance to the here and now. For example, in the case of initiation, if the result of the ritual were that the initiates had become part of an enduring entity in the 'other world', this entity would have no political significance.

In fact, in the cases examined in this book, a solution seems to be found which rejoins the here and now and the transcendental units which the rituals create. At first sight, this solution appears to be simply a contradiction of the move into the other world since it is a return into this world. However, as we shall see, the contradiction is avoided by making the return into this world something quite different from the departure from it. In the first part of the ritual the here and now is simply left behind by the move towards the transcendental. This initial movement represents the transcendental as supremely desirable and the here and now as of no value. The return is different. In the return the transcendental is not left behind but continues to be attached to those who made the initial move in its direction; its value is not negated. Secondly, the return to the here and now is really a conquest of the here and now by the transcendental. In the case of initiation, the initiate does not merely return to the world he had left behind. He is a changed person, a permanently transcendental person who can therefore dominate the here and now of which he previously was a part.

The return is therefore a conquest of the kind of thing which had been abandoned but, as if to mark the difference between the going and the coming back, the actual identity of the vital here and now is altered. Vitality is regained, but it is not the home-grown native vitality which was discarded in the first part of the rituals that is regained, but, instead, a conquered vitality obtained from *outside* beings, usually animals, but sometimes plants, other peoples or women. In ritual representations, native vitality is replaced by a conquered, external, consumed vitality. It is through this substitution that an image is created in which humans can leave this life and join the transcendental, yet still not be alienated from the here and now. They become part of permanent institutions, and as superior beings they can reincorporate the present life through the idiom of conquest or consumption.

If the rituals dramatise a journey of the person to the beyond and a conquering return, this mirrors a similar two-way experience which is felt as taking place inside the person. The first part of the rituals involves an experiential dichotomisation of the subjects into an over-vital side and a transcendental side. Then, as in the external drama, the transcendental drives out the vital so that the person becomes, for a time, entirely transcendental. This victory of one side of the person over the other is what requires the first element of violence in the rituals.

This violence is, however, only a preliminary to a subsequent violence which involves the triumphant experiential recovery of vitality into the person by the transcendental element. However (and again as in the external drama), this recovery of vitality does not compromise the superiority of the transcendental identity, because the recovered vitality is mastered by the transcendental.

Unlike the native vitality of the first stage which must be driven out of oneself, the vitality reintroduced in the second stage is taken from external sources and is consumed as the food of the transcendental subject, often literally through the mouth. This second violence can therefore be considered as the consequence of the first; it is the elimination of ordinary vitality which necessitates its replacement by a new, plundered vitality, and the contact with the transcendental which provides the impetus for this forced substitution. The whole ritual process can therefore be understood as the construction of a form of 'rebounding violence' both at the public and at the experiential level.

In some ways this argument is similar to the old model usually attributed to Van Gennep for rites of passage; in other ways it is different (Van Gennep 1909). Van Gennep stressed how actors pass from a stage where they are separated from society, to a liminal state, to a stage where they are reintegrated into society. I retain the idea of the three stages but I attribute to them quite a different content. While Van Gennep sees the drama of the first stage as a separation between the primary actor and the group he or she leaves behind, I see it principally as a dramatically constructed dichotomisation located within the body of each of the participants. The second stage for Van Gennep, and even more for Turner, is a period of liminality quite separate from the rest of the sequence (Turner 1969). Here it is seen as the moment when the initiate is given the transcendental part of his identity which will dominate for the rest of his life. Finally, Van Gennep describes the third stage as a reintegration into society, and Turner as a reintegration into the mundane world. Here the third stage is not seen as a return to the condition left behind in the first stage but as an aggressive consumption of a vitality which is *different* in origin from that which had originally been lost.

Van Gennep and Turner have little to say about violence. In so far as they recognise it, it is a mark of the initial stage of separation. They completely miss the significance of the much more dramatic violence of the return to the mundane. For me, however, this conquering and consuming is central because it is what explains the political outcomes of religious action. First of all, it needs to be violent, otherwise the subordination of vitality would not be demonstrated. Secondly, this final consumption is outwardly directed towards other species. In many of the examples discussed we shall see how the consumption of animals, for example, can be represented as merely a preliminary to expansionist violence against neighbours.

The book argues, therefore, that in the core ritual structure which it identifies, the sequence which leads to 'rebounding violence', there lies an explanation of the symbolism of violence present in so many religious phenomena. Furthermore, it argues that there also lies the explanation of the often-noted fact that religion so easily furnishes an idiom of expansionist violence to people in a whole range of societies, an idiom which, under certain circumstances, becomes a legitimation for actual violence.

Such a conclusion may seem close to that reached by such writers as Girard

(1972) and Burkert (1983), who see an indissoluble link between violence and religion, but it does so for totally different reasons. These writers assume an innate aggressiveness in humans which is expressed, and to a certain extent purged, by ritual. In contrast I do not base myself on some innate propensity to violence but argue that violence is itself a result of the attempt to create the transcendental in religion and politics.

Much of the content of this book was originally presented as four lectures commemorating the great American anthropologist Lewis Henry Morgan, and although dealing with topics which were not his immediate concerns I hope the book follows in his tradition. In fact, I believe that a consideration of the relation between the religious and the political would have interested Lewis Henry Morgan for a number of reasons.

Firstly, even though he wrote very little about religion as such, Morgan was possibly the greatest exponent of what has always characterised anthropology, that is the demonstration that aspects of life which other human sciences choose to separate are fundamentally interconnected. Secondly, Morgan never disguised the fact that his aim was to understand how human societies have become the kind of phenomena they are in a way which both places human beings in the wider processes of evolution and recognises the unique implications of human psychology for human evolution. Thirdly, this book deals with one of Morgan's central concerns: understanding the way in which human beings can create representations of seemingly permanent institutions, such as what Morgan called the clan or the gens, against the lived experience of their own mortality and the discontinuous biological processes of human life. Finally, in returning to very basic questions of anthropology, which inevitably have evolutionary implications, I am quite consciously following Morgan's lead. Morgan recognised that this kind of study could not escape a consideration of the moral implications of human social evolution, since anthropologists, like other human scientists, are peculiar in that for them the observer and the observed are ultimately identical.

A number of recent writers have argued that cross-cultural theory inevitably involves the author in an arrogant domination of the subject being discussed. This does not seem to me to be true. Rather, it is the self-conscious refusal to engage in attempts at explanation which I feel is the danger for the anthropologist. Like Morgan, I believe that to propose a theory is to implicate ourselves as much as other peoples in the explanation. The continuing value of Morgan's work today seems to me to show that it is only by attempting to understand in this way that we can move on, even if the conclusions reached are provisional and incomplete. It is surely by this essay into understanding that we acknowledge our connectedness with and involvement in the world, and the continuity between our own and other societies.

2

Initiation

One of the better-known groups of people in modern anthropology are the Orokaiva of Papua New Guinea. This is partly because they have been so well described by a number of anthropologists, especially F. E. Williams, and partly because the ethnography has been subtly reanalysed by, among others, Schwimmer, and above all by Iteanu, who has recently published a brilliant, careful and convincing reanalysis of the available material. In this chapter I use Iteanu's work to flesh out the very abstract outline of rebounding violence which was given in the previous chapter. In particular I follow Iteanu's analysis of Orokaiva initiation, which acts out the transformation which gives this book its title: the transformation of initiates from prey into hunters. However, in the end, this chapter reaches very different theoretical conclusions from those of Iteanu and a brief discussion of these differences will serve to define and advance the argument.

Like so many peoples around the world the Orokavia practise the kind of rituals which have been called 'initiations' in anthropological literature. This is because passing through these rituals is considered an essential step to beginning or continuing life as a full moral person. The initiation ritual of the Orokavia is reminiscent of that of many other peoples and is typical of the part of New Guinea in which they live. This local character is nowhere clearer than in the fact that the ritual seems to be concerned as much with pigs, birds and spirits as it is with the human beings it initiates. It differs from other New Guinea initiation rituals, however, in that the initiates are both girls and boys. Although I ignore the significance of this fact in this chapter, I shall return to it in chapter 5, which deals with the relevance of gender for the issues concerned in this book.

At the time set for the ritual the first important act is that the Orokaiva village is invaded from the outside by people who have been hiding, lurking in the encircling bush. These people wear masks decorated with bird feathers and pigs' tusks, behave in ways which are reminiscent of birds and imitate the sound made by birds. The masked actors represent spirits, especially the ancestral spirits of dead people of the village. These masked intruders, shouting that they are spirits, arrive as if from the forest and chase the children, maltreating them. The intruders are terrifying; they advance biting and assaulting trees and pigs, and shouting in the direction of the children 'Bite, bite, bite'.[1] Meanwhile the parents beg the spirits not to 'kill' the children. As Iteanu points out, the intruders act as though they were hunters stalking wild pigs. In fact they are seeking the children who are to be initiated, but the image of the pig hunt is continued as they chase the children hither and thither, before finally herding them onto a platform reminiscent of the ones on which dead bodies may be placed and of the type on which pigs are killed, cut up and distributed at major rituals.

It is not difficult to imagine that the whole proceeding must be extremely frightening for the initiates but this is also true for their parents. The reason is that it is believed that the ritual may very possibly lead to the death of the children and Iteanu assures us that this indeed happens not infrequently. This means that in agreeing to let their children be initiated and in participating in the proceedings the adults are willingly submitting to an attack on their children and by extension on themselves. This co-operation with an external attack which often involves, as here, a notion of penetration, whether this be bodily or geographical, is an essential element of the pattern this book examines.

The initial pig hunt may be a symbolic representation of the killing of the children, but at least at this stage of the proceedings the children do not die. What happens after they have been driven onto the platform is that they are covered in a blinding cape and taken out of the village to an isolated hut in the bush where they are forbidden to eat normal food, where they are not allowed to wash or speak aloud and from where they are not allowed to look out. In the initiation hut the children are told that by now they too have become spirits of the dead. This is because becoming a spirit is what the Orokaiva believe happens after death and the children have gone through a process which mimics their 'death'. After all, they have been hunted as though they were pigs, taken to a platform of the kind on which pigs are killed, cut up and their meat distributed and they, like the dead, have lost their individuality, their sense of sight and their power of audible and articulate speech.

In the initiation huts the initiates are thus symbolically dead and can therefore be considered to have become spirits. There they undergo various ordeals and are taught a number of secrets. Above all they are shown the feathers of the masks they will be able to wear as initiated adults. The Orokaiva say that during the seclusion the initiates' feathers 'grow' on them. There the initiates are taught to play the sacred flutes and bull roarers that are represented as the 'voices' of the spirits. They are also taught spirit dances, which only initiated persons can know and perform. One can therefore say that from the time of their initiation to their real death the Orokaiva will remain partly spirits and this transformation will be manifested by their right to put on spirit masks to make the spirits be heard through the playing of flutes and bull roarers, and to represent, or perhaps be, spirits in rituals such as initiation.

After a considerable time of seclusion in the initiation hut the initiates return to the village apparently quite transformed. A key element of this transformation is the relation of the initiates to pigs. Previously, the last time they were in the village, the children had been ritually killed at the hands of the masked adults as though they were pigs. Now, after their sojourn in the initiation hut, the initiates, who have partly become spirits themselves, return not as prey but as hunters of pigs, shouting the same formula which had been addressed to them 'Bite, bite, bite'. Iteanu puts the matter thus: 'from having been victims the children have become murderers of these other "children" who are in fact pigs' (Iteanu 1983: 111). This transformation is marked by much of the symbolism which makes hunters of the initiated children and also, as we shall see, killers. This is literally so in the case of the initiation described by Chinnery and Beaver (1915), where the first act required of the emergent children is that they must participate in a pig hunt.[2] In all cases the symbolism of the initiate as a hunter-cum-warrior is underlined by the triumphant dance they perform on returning to the village and above all by the fact that they climb on to a similar platform to which they had been driven as hunted pigs, and where they now strut, themselves distributing the meat of killed pigs. This time, however, it is real pigs which have been hunted and real meat which is offered.

The completion of the transformation of prey into hunter is clear for all to see. At the beginning the children were taken on to the platform as hunted pigs by masked and feathered intruders representing spirits who shouted 'Bite, bite, bite'. Now shouting the very same words, dressed in the feather masks which have grown on them, representing the spirits which they have in part become, they distribute the meat of hunted and killed pigs.[3]

Anthropologists have long been familiar with the general pattern of initiation rituals which this Orokaiva example follows, although, as Iteanu points out, they have often tended to concentrate on the supposed social or psychological functions these rituals might fulfil, rather than on the content of the symbolism or on what the actors say the rituals are about. Nonetheless the contention that the transformation of the initiates from victims into killers is a typical aspect of these rituals is one which ought to be easily accepted by most scholars in the field.

In this book, however, it is my intention to propose that this simple pattern applies well beyond initiation and has much greater significance for our understanding of the nature of human beings than it does merely as a recurrent feature of a special type of ritual. The dramatic transformation of prey into hunter, which we saw among the Orokaiva, underlies in different forms the practices which can easily be subsumed under the English word 'religion', as well as many practices which cannot. I shall argue that sacrifice, spirit possession, fertility rituals and funerals contain the same underlying core of the transformation of prey into hunter as initiation and that this pattern is also present in state ceremonies, in certain aspects of politics, as well as in the ideas which underlie the rules of incest and exogamy and some of the representations of gender.

But before such wide-ranging issues are considered it is necessary to understand some aspects of Orokaiva initiation better. In the ritual three sorts of beings are involved: spirits, humans and pigs. The prominence of pigs in a ritual which is intended to make children into full, responsible moral beings may at first be somewhat surprising and we need to know more about the Orokaiva to understand how they see these animals and what their attitude to pigs is, though in this they are similar to many other New Guinea and Melanesian peoples (Modjeska 1982).

One of the first elements for understanding the Orokaiva symbolical significance of pigs, and more particularly domesticated pigs,[4] is their perceived similarity to humans, a point rightly emphasised by Schwimmer, who discusses one of a number of myths which seem to deal with the uncertain differentiation of pigs and humans (Schwimmer 1973: 140), and especially by Iteanu. This perception of similarity is partly due to the fact that, since there are no other large mammals in Papua New Guinean villages, pigs stand out as the animal species closest by far to humans in their mode of reproduction. It also comes from the fact that pigs live in, or rather under, houses, in very close proximity to women and children and that they eat much the same food as humans.[5] It is, however, more particularly the similarity between piglets and human children which the Orokaiva choose to stress.[6] Piglets are often suckled by Orokaiva women together with human children. The Orokaiva call pigs the 'children' of their owners and talk of a pig's mother to refer to the person who has brought it up.[7]

But Orokaiva symbolism also stresses another connection between pigs and humans: pigs are like humans because pigs die. Of course all animals die, but much of Orokaiva symbolism particularly stresses pig mortality. The very place where pigs live, under the house, associates them with human death since this is where corpses are placed. All pigs, however lovable (and New Guinea ethnographies often record the deep affection that exists between humans and their pigs), are ultimately destined to be slaughtered. This is done very publicly at rituals, right in the middle of villages. The omnipresence of pigs in New Guinea villages is therefore also a declaration and an emphasis of the presence of death in everyday life: rather like the black-clad widows of the Mediterranean, pigs inform all activities with the inseparability of human life and death. Other writers on New Guinea make similar points: thus Hirsch (1987) also stresses the same contrast I am drawing here between pigs and birds and therefore qualifies pigs as 'over-mortal'. At the same time he also notes the connection between pigs and children by pointing out how similar the sounds made by piglets and human babies are.

The promised slaughter of pigs at rituals is both the glorious fulfilment of their destiny and a moment of real sadness. This sadness is recognised and marked by the fact that the human 'parents' of the slaughtered pig publicly mourn and weep for their 'child' when it is killed in a ritual as though it were a real child.[8] Thus for the Orokaiva pigs are 'almost children' who are about to be slaughtered, and this combination of child and victim is the key to their ritual significance.

If the Orokaiva stress the similarities of pigs and humans, they also stress the difference between pigs and humans. This difference concerns above all the relation of humans to spirits because, since humans can be represented as pigs which have been conquered and moulded by spirits, this cannot, or rather should not, happen to pigs. Pigs are, or should be, like humans but without any trace of a spirit element.[9] Before we move on to a discussion of the difference between pigs and humans it is therefore necessary to understand Orokaiva ideas about spirits.

Orokaiva beliefs about spirits are unformulated and this caused much bewilderment to early ethnographers (Williams 1930: 260). For them there are many kinds of spirits, but the most important are the spirits of the dead of a particular village or clan. Williams tells us that 'Orokaiva religion concerns itself primarily with the spirits of the dead' (1930: 268). The spirits of the dead are normally localised in the bush, more particularly in a village of the dead in a remote place. Although they are without pig-like mortal bodies, ancestral spirits are nonetheless very much like people. Spirits have language, though normally inaudible; they have personality and motivation. They should be concerned about the welfare of their descent groups in the world of the living.

It could be said that, for the Orokaiva, spirits have all the attributes of humans *except* those attributes which human share with domesticated pigs, attributes such as bodies, grease, sexuality and death. In fact the main difference between spirits on the one hand, and humans and pigs on the other, is that spirits do not die. Williams tells us that the Orokaiva word for spirit means 'the being who survives death' (Williams 1930: 267). Just as pigs can be said to be represented in Orokaiva symbolism as over-mortal, spirits are represented as immortal or rather non-mortal.

In fact the categorical contrast between pig mortality and spirit immortality is represented and dramatised every time an Orokaiva kills a pig. Just as he is about to strike, the hunter says the name of a spirit, usually a dead forebear, and he thereby identifies himself with the spirit. He thus evokes, for an instant, an immortal in deadly opposition with the pig which is being killed (Williams 1925: 417).[10] Ancestral spirits exist fully and freely only after the death of humans, while pigs only exist before death. Thus in the matter of death, pigs and spirits are symmetrical opposites to each other.

This temporal contrast takes on an even more graphic form as a spatial contrast. The domestic pigs which will be killed in rituals are closely associated with houses and villages, especially the underneath of houses where they live. Spirits, on the other hand, live in the bush. This spatial contrast also reflects a contrast in the pig's and spirit's relation to the transformative processes of life. Villages are places from which productive and reproductive activities are organised. They are places where the young grow up and where the adults grow old. The underneaths of houses in villages, the homes of pigs, are in many ways the very epicentre of all this, since they are places where corpses and sometimes placenta will be buried.

On the other hand, the bush, or rather the forest, the home of spirits, is for the Orokaiva, rather like the location of the biblical lilies of the field, away from work, daily care and ageing. The opposition between the location of domesticated pigs and of spirits comes dramatically to life in the ritual discussed above. However, before the full significance of the movement from the village to the bush and back again can be considered there is another element in the representation of spirits which must be dealt with.

Although the Orokaiva do not explicitly associate spirits with birds as do so many other New Guinea peoples (Gillison 1980; Hirsch 1987), the represent-ation of the spirits in rituals such as initiation is predominantly as bird-like. The most important features of the masks of the people representing the spirits in the rituals are feathers and, as noted above, acquiring the right to wear a spirit mask by the initiates is spoken of as 'growing feathers'. Again, the noise which the spirits make imitates bird calls. Finally, some of the dances of spirits are probably imitating the actions of birds, since this is the case almost throughout New Guinea.[11]

I would argue that this visual and auditory avian image of the spirits in rituals is much more significant than the unwillingly answered questions of ethnographers about what spirits are like, though it is likely that we are dealing with an idea which normally need not take an exegetical form. The image of the spirits in the ritual firmly represents them as being creatures of the 'above', in opposition to pigs which are, as we saw, of the 'underneath', something which is again visually confirmed in the ritual and is noted by Iteanu (1983). Furthermore this association of spirits with birds may have yet another implication. New Guinea beliefs about birds are very complex but often (Lewis 1980; Hirsch 1987) in other parts of New Guinea, and also probably among the Orokaiva, they are believed to be creatures beyond the processes of ageing or even to be immortal. This aspect of birds would thus underline once again the contrast between the over-mortal pigs and the spirits which 'survive death'.

Finally, we must turn to the third creatures alluded to in the ritual: humans. Humans are like both pigs and spirits. We have already seen how humans, especially young humans, are like domesticated pigs because they live most of the time in villages and are mortal. Both humans and pigs share in a necessary involvement with the dialectics of impermanent life. It must be remembered, however, that there is also a way in which Orokaiva humans, at least initiated humans, are also like spirits, or bird-like, and can therefore be immortal, feral and beyond process.

The spirit aspect of humans is manifest in the fact that, unlike pigs, they can represent spirits in rituals such as the ritual of initiation. Williams interestingly argues that this is no mere 'representation' but that the masked actors *are*, in a sense and for a while, what the costumes they wear represent. *For a while* they truly believe themselves to be spirits and birds at the very same time that they know they are masquerading. I shall return to this point in the next chapter.

Because they are partly spirits and birds, initiated humans, unlike domesticated pigs, have another home in addition to that of the village. They, like birds and spirits, also have a home in the bush, and this is literally true, since after initiation Orokaivans can spend time in the cult house located in the forest. For the Orokaivans living humans are therefore dual beings with two homes: one side of them is pig-like and located in the village and one side of them is spirit- or bird-like and located in the bush, but because of their duality, they are not really fully at home in either place. They lead a double life, partly in the village where they live like pigs, and also on occasion partly in the bush, where they can anticipate death in the village and be for a while totally spirit.

The spirit-like aspect of humans comes from their relationship to the spirits of the dead which is re-established at initiation.[12] Thus we are inevitably forced to consider briefly the tangled question of the nature of Orokaivan descent. The clans which writers such as Williams identified are very difficult to define as they incorporate elements of unilineal descent, elements of locality and an element of being part of the following of a living or dead big man. Their day-to-day importance is so slight that Schwimmer refused to recognise them as descent groups at all. What they are above all, as Iteanu suggests, is a relationship of certain living people to certain dead spirits which were associated with the village of the living. There is a sense, therefore, that the establishment of this relationship in a ritual such as Orokaivan initiation is what makes descent. These clans are not groups as they would be understood by a sociologist, but are, rather, mystical groups which concern only one side of existence. These groups are evoked in the bush and when rituals are performed, because then people can forget for a moment that they are mortal or village humans and can see themselves as pure spirits or birds, at one with the spirits of the dead and, like them, immortal. In the bush people are momentarily freed from their pig-like practical existence bound by the productive processes of the gardens and the domestic reproductive cycles of birth and inevitable village death.

With this background we can now understand the first part of Orokaiva initiation. The young, reared in the village through the same processes as domesticated pigs, suckled and nurtured in much the same way, looking and sounding much like piglets, must, as they grow up, gain their bird-like aspect and discover their new spirit home in the bush. This occurs when the elders call in the death-bringing spirits, encouraging them to invade the village and take their children into the bush. If they are to be born as spirits the initiates must first die as pigs so that their post-mortal existence as spirits, that is as members of the clan, can begin. This explains why the adults allow and co-operate with the invasion of their village by the masked spirits and the killing of their children. This is a form of killing which is usually merely symbolic, but is also always potentially real, since, as noted above, deaths sometimes do occur during the ritual seclusion. It is a great deal to have to submit to so that order and continuity can be created.

Not only does this analysis explain many of the attributes of this particular ritual, but it would also be applicable to many other rituals which have been called initiations in the literature, since the features I have just discussed are precisely those which anthropologists have emphasised as most characteristic of initiation generally. For example, the spatial movement of initiation which informed Van Gennep's pioneering study can be seen in terms of the duality of modes of existence created in such a representation (1909). The same is true of the animal symbolism which is a common feature of initiation rituals. We can also understand what is probably one of the most common assertions concerning initiation in the anthropological literature, that initiation rituals employ the symbolism of killing, funerals and murderous violence to bring about a form of rebirth.

But all these well-known features of initiation rituals only concern the first part of the ritual under study and, for that matter, the first part of most initiation rituals. The second half, the return to the village and the real aggressive consumption, must also be understood, and here the classical analyses of anthropology are much less help.

Anthropologists trained in the Durkheimian tradition have seen this second stage, the return, as merely the reintegration of the initiate into society after a temporary separation. Of course there is a sense in which this is true, but understanding the process in this way also misses the point and even makes this re-entry paradoxical. What would be the point of leaving one form of existence behind with such panache merely to return to it? To use the words Durkheim would have used, why leave the profane and enter the sacred at such cost, only to return to the profane?

The answer to such a question is that in fact initiates never again fully leave the sacred but that they achieve a combination of the sacred and the profane which is of a very special hierarchical kind.[13] In the Orokaiva case this can be seen as we look again at the ritual representation of humans as partly pig-like and partly spirit-like. If mortal, pig-like village existence can be escaped by dying as a village pig and becoming a bird-like spirit, this cannot be a complete solution for living humans, especially young living humans. The children cannot become full-time spirits, permanently located in the bush, since they would then be dead. They must also stay alive in the village environment with pigs and domesticity, with agriculture and with birth and death. In other words, while people are alive, it is *by definition* impossible to escape completely to the world of the spirits. It is only possible to do this occasionally by anticipating death, and then only for a little while before one must go back to the living.

But here another problem arises: How is it possible to avoid this return being simply a negation of the escape to the spirits which was the point of the first part of the ritual? How is it possible for this not to be a humiliating retreat back to the pigs? In fact the ritual contains a symbolic resolution to this fundamental problem and it is a resolution that we find again and again in different contexts in different societies. If they are to continue as living human beings, that complex indeterminacy between pig and spirit, the initiates, having become pure bird spirits in the bush, must then regain their pig aspect for village life, but (and this is the essential point) *not in the same way as before*.

Before initiation the pig in the children was 'given' in their nature, it was internal, it was nurtured and grown as the children were raised in the same way that pigs were raised, and so to get rid of the symbolic pig in the ritual the opposite had to be done to it: it had to be frightened, hunted and killed by the conquering spirits. But when the children return from their time spent in the bush as spirits they must regain the pig element in the form of conquered food, for example the meat of the real pigs which have really been threatened and killed. This regained pig element is therefore not identical to the internal pig which had been violently taken from them in the first part of the ritual. Now, in the second half of the ritual, it is external pig which they incorporate. Actually in most cases it is doubly external pig which they eat as a result of the hunt, since the pig flesh so obtained is exchanged with affinal partners who will ultimately return pig reared and killed by them in their villages. It is this substitution of native internal pig for conquered external pig which ensures that there is no contradiction, but that instead we appear to have a forward movement as the transcendental remains uncompromised but is still the beneficiary of vitality.

Indeed it is only when we bear in mind the significance of the exchange of pig meat for building up political alliances and followings as well as for obtaining wives that we fully grasp what is evoked in a culture such as this by the recovery of external pig meat in exchange for the loss of natal pig. Pig meat thus comes to stand for strength in this world, which is believed to come not only from the nutritional effect of the meat, especially the fat,[14] but also from strength-giving political and affinal exchange relationships which are created and maintained by the exchange of pork.

After the ritual the initiates are as they will be for the rest of their lives, a mixture of pig and spirit, but now the spirit or clan or bird element dominates the pig element. This is because this new pig element is a conquered substance, the result of the internalisation of the external food of the 'spirit'. In this way the reintroduction of the pig element into the person is not a humiliating return to the original pre-initiation state from which the initiates had started; rather it is dramatised as a triumphal move forward.

In addition, it should not be forgotten, as is so often done, that initiation involves many other people as well as the initiates. If we put the whole matter from the point of view of the adults at the initiation ritual we can see that, in initiating their children, the adults have allowed their children to be killed, consumed and conquered by the spirits, just as they themselves were once killed and consumed at their own initiation, in order that these children will become successful hunters, killers, consumers and conquerors of their environment and of the future.

But the connection of the adults and the initiates is much more intimate than this. Symbolically, emotionally and physically all the villagers accompany the children in their journey from the village to the bush; all therefore become, to a degree, hunted pigs or prey, and all are assimilated to the children as they return as hunters. All are therefore, as Iteanu repeatedly points out, conquered and conquering. Or to put it another way, although in the initial hunt the adults of the village are associated with the invading spirits (after all it is they who represent them), there is also an element of themselves which is being chased round the village, since it is their children, part of themselves, who are hunted. Like the children, the adults are both hunted and hunters. And this is even true of the spirits. Like the children, they were driven into the bush by death, and like the children they will also return to the village as hunters. This will occur at the next initiation, when the masks will represent them violently crossing back over the boundary between the bush and the village.

All human generations, past, present and future, are therefore involved in this oscillating progressing spiral between bush and village, hunted and hunter, pig and spirit, both in the initiation ritual and always.

This construction, or rather reconstruction, of the ritual representation of the composition of the Orokaiva is revealed by the costume of the mature actors in ritual. As Strathern and O'Hanlon have shown, costumes in New Guinea are a revelation of the inner self (Strathern 1979; O'Hanlon 1983). They are a kind of display of the internal person disclosed if by X-ray. The costume is above all bird-like, but it also contains elements from pigs, especially the tusks which are a sign of their strength. Unlike the feathers of the costume which have 'grown' on the masked dancers, the pig elements are seen as parts of hunted and captured pigs. The mask, therefore, shows the person as having been first conquered by the spirits so as to become a spirit and, as a result, having subsequently become a successful hunter of powerful pigs which give the wearer the controlled strength of the pigs.[15]

There is, however, yet a further element to the pig hunt and the menacing dance display which marks the initiates' return to the village. As in other parts of New Guinea where such rituals end in an aggressive removal of the peace-maintaining boundary symbol between one's own group and outsiders (Rappaport 1984: 125), an act which is a formal declaration of war, Orokaiva initiation concludes with an open-ended menace to outsiders which can in certain circumstances be the beginning of serious hostility.

The pig hunt in which the initiates participate after their seclusion is not the only aggressive act enjoined on the children on their return. After the concluding displays the male initiates are presented with a decoration called *otohu*, which has been the subject of considerable discussion. Beaver, in 1918, in a report cited by Williams (1930: 177ff., 203), saw *otohu* as 'homicidal emblems' which were given to a successful slayer of an enemy. He noted, however, that *otohu* could also be obtained at rituals such as initiation in return for the gift of a slaughtered pig. Beaver argued, therefore, that there were two kinds of *otohu*. Williams, in contrast, convincingly argues that there is no sharp distinction between the two types (1930: 203ff.) and in this he is, by and large, followed by Schwimmer and Iteanu. In fact the identity between Beaver's two types of *otohu* indicates once again how pigs and humans are interchangeable in certain contexts. The final pig hunt of the ritual becomes a symbolic war on outsiders and that is how Iteanu sees it. The way the *otohu* is given is even more revealing. It is offered by an elderly man who has been a famous killer in his time. Before indirectly giving the *otohu* he recites the names of his past victims to the children, who are thereby encouraged to become killers in their turn. The pig hunt is thus revealed to be the first stage in an ever-amplifying hunt against neighbours and enemies.

Of course when the Orokaiva are militarily weak this element is mere rhetoric and only pigs can be killed in fulfilment of the two-way movement, in and out, of the world of death. But when the situation looks good and the neighbours are weak, the murderous oratory marks the beginning of real military killing expeditions, which are seen, as Iteanu makes clear, in the same idiom as ceremonial and matrimonial exchange, a point to which I shall return in the third chapter.

The place of the pigs in the hunt and the dances of the emerging initiates is therefore interchangeable with that of killed enemies, who in the past were also eaten, and it is no accident that the same word is used by the Orokaiva for the killing of pigs and humans and for no other living beings.[16] When the military situation makes this possible, the initiates should not be satisfied with the poor substitute for enemies represented by the pigs but should become true killers earning their *otohu* fully. This fact, seen clearly by Iteanu, makes us understand better the allegorical role of pigs in the symbolism. As argued above, they represent human vitality and strength without the spirit element introduced by initiation. However, the pigs remain part metaphor for that external vitality which must be conquered and consumed and part reality. When events have made it possible the logic of rebounding violence can be fuller and more literal: then it is conquered human outsiders, people whose spirits have either been beaten or who have been abandoned by them, who can be killed and consumed.

This extension of ritual violence beyond the ritual itself concerns only the second aspect of rebounding violence, that is the reconquest of external vitality. The first violent element, the attack against internal vitality, has little political significance outside the ritual itself except as a preliminary to the second element. However, it should be noted that the very form of the ritual lends itself to this turning outwards of its concluding section. This is because the final ritual act of consumption is physically real, is directed towards the external world and often takes the form of an invasion of that world.

Indeed the centrality of the military and aggressive aspects of Orokaiva initiation seems confirmed in yet another way. The performances of Orokaiva initiation ritual were interrupted for a period from about 1930 until the independence of Papua New Guinea, when they were resumed on a wide scale and included large numbers of older initiates who had not been through the ceremony at the usual age. As Iteanu himself notes, one of the reasons for the timing of the disappearance and reappearance of initiation was that the colonially imposed end to warfare had made the ritual unsuitable, while the resumption of warfare revived it.

With the conclusion of the ritual in its display of symbolic violence, which can become actual warfare, we have the complete sequence of rebounding violence. The basis of this process has been the Orokaiva ritual representation of the division of the person between two elements, one consuming the other, expressed in initiation and costume. This is an apparent solution to the problem which, I suggest, most societies attempt to resolve: how human beings can be the constituent elements of permanent institutional structures. To achieve this they must appear, in a certain light at least, to be immortal and unchanging, and therefore other than human; at the same time, they must also be truly alive, in a human body which cannot but be perceived as transformative and mortal. The construction of the ritual drama of rebounding violence is an attempt to avoid the force of this contradiction. Although in fact this attempt can never be entirely successful, the reason why this image can seem to be a resolution to the fundamental problem, the different ways in which this representation of rebounding conquest is achieved, and the personal and political implications of these rituals are the main concerns of this book.

Biological and social reproduction depends on the creation of a chain of individuals who are born, nurtured and die and in which the young replace the old. In this system, what is left of the old and the dead, that is, principally what they have created, is taken by the young for their own purposes. Thus, ultimately, the experience of life is that the young conquer the old and consume their product.

In contrast to this representation of life, a ritual such as Orokaiva initiation totally reverses the value of this reality. In the first part the community is promised permanence if it is willing to allow its young to 'die' at the hands of 'ancestors', who actually expel the initiates from the place of life and thus appear to outlive them. Continuity is apparently achieved by death replacing birth. In the second part of the ritual the young return, but this is not a reversal of the first part because by then the initiates are representing the dead and they are under the leadership of elders. The return of the initiates is therefore represented as merely a continuation of what has happened before. Once again it is the 'ancestors' who break into the place of life and conquer it. The flow continues in the same direction. These 'young' ancestors admittedly recover their vitality but this causes no reversal, since when they recover it it lacks autonomy and is from outside. Of course if these new spirits were to recover their own natal vitality, then the flow would be reversed, but the presence of other beings who, unlike the initiates, can be conquered once and for all, ensures the completion of the image of death conquering life at the cost of externalising the successions of conquests. The presence of an alien species, the pigs, is therefore essential to the construction of apparently life-transcending human institutions. They ensure that vitality can be both abandoned and regained without contradiction, since as absolute victims, the pigs, unlike the initiates, will not be able to conquer in their turn and so will ensure that the direction of the conquest is not reversed.

In this way the symbolism of the ritual creates a counter-image to village-centred, dialectical, biological and economic reproduction by inverting it. For the Orokaiva, entering this spirit world where generations succeed each other in the opposite way to the everyday world takes the form of leaving the village for the bush, where a mirror-like alternative existence is set up. There, birth and nurturing are the waste products of a life one lives thanks to death.[17] In the world of ritual, existence is literally transcendent; it is a world 'on the other side'.

But, inevitably for the living, this is a world which can only be entered some of the time since one cannot leave the world where birth is creative and death is destructive without actually dying. This means that both existence in the village, where the young replace the old, *and* existence in the bush, where the old replace the young, must be combined. This duality itself has two sides. In terms of external events this combination is achieved by an alternation between periods of ritual and periods of ordinary life. But the temporal and spatial duality of Orokaiva social life must also have a referent internal to the person and the community since the person and the community are always participating in both flows. Thus we have the ritual representation of humans as part pig and part spirit. The pig element is caught in the flow where the young replace the old and the spirit element in the opposite flow where the old replace the young.

Now there is no evidence of course for believing that most of the time the Orokaiva would normally have any occasion to express this analytical view of the self, or that it has psychological significance in daily life, but in rituals, where the contradiction is acted upon, it becomes objectified emblematically in certain ways such as the costumes of the masks combining bird and pig elements. Indeed it is the parallel of the internal relation between prey and hunter with the external drama which gives the Orokaiva ritual of initiation its power. This complex internal/external analogue is crucial to all the phenomena with which this book is concerned, and I shall discuss it more fully in the next chapter.

The combination in one body and one community of the two opposite modes of existence is more problematic than the temporal sequencing of periods of ritual and periods without ritual. It is as if the person, previously living as a pig on an escalator going one way, were being invited to step with one foot on to another escalator going the other way. This dilemma, which applies both to the individual and to the community as a whole, is, as the image of the escalators shows, a perilous situation.

The statement that the Orokaiva think of the person as part pig and part spirit would miss the point in yet another way. It suggests a static combination, while what we are dealing with is the combination of two processes. One process is moved forward in time by birth, maturation, productive activity, and is represented by pigs, while the other process is moved forward by death and conquest as it continually consumes the continually growing pig element.

This representation of continuing consumption of the vital by the transcendental is the way the spirit element can appear as permanent in a continually transforming living community, and how such social institutions, which are made up of transcendental persons, can therefore appear as present and alive. The process is as follows: the person is represented as symbolically dual, with one side chaotic but vital and the other superior and transcendental. Then, the two parts are set in motion one against the other so that the one is, often literally, disappearing into the mouth of the other, thereby producing an image of a permanent order which nonetheless contains vitality. The consuming element was originally defined by opposition to the vital as the moral, superior aspect of the person. This is what remains beyond the processes inherent in any individual. It remains unchanged but it swallows up vitality. Thus the moral entity remains both a particular living unit and also an impersonal part of a transcendent order. In this way the central puzzle of the creation of the apparently permanent out of the transformative is phenomenologically achieved. This creation is apparently necessary for all social systems which rely on the illusion of an institutional framework transcending individuals; and nearly all societies in the world do this.

The inevitability of this construction also explains the other central theme of this book: the presence of the idiom of violence in the phenomena under discussion. For such a construction to operate there is a need for a double violence or a 'rebounding' violence. There is the need for the violence of expulsion of the native vital element and the need for the successive violence of the consumption of external vitality. These different elements of violence necessarily imply each other. Because of the parallelism of the internal process and the external drama of the ritual this rebounding violence also has two sides, one internal to the person and invisible, and one external and highly visible, and it is this parallelism which gives the ritual its emotional force.

Finally, this emotionally charged, outwardly directed consumption and violence in the ritual and the person is what, as we have seen, leads to the non-ritual, political implications of the proceedings. The full significance of this ritual and political culmination, however, comes in part from the fact that the violence of the external ritual coincides with the invisible internal process.

To clarify the theoretical status of this discussion it is useful to contrast briefly what has been said with the theories of Iteanu, who has been my primary guide to the ethnography of the Orokaiva and whom I have largely followed only to reach categorically opposed conclusions.

Iteanu demonstrates very convincingly how all the rituals he analyses (and of course he covers much more than initiation) establish relations of exchange between humans and spirits, between different humans belonging to different groups, between animals and men. For him these various networks of exchanges create a ritual totality which gives meaning to every act and value of the Orokaiva. He sees this whole as greater than the parts and for him the whole is the ritual system. It is this holistic ritual system which is for Iteanu the sole source of meaning of the different aspects of Orokaiva ritual and culture.

In contrast I have argued that, far from the ritual system being an organising totality, it only has sense and power because it is based on an image of reproduction which originates quite outside the ritual process in an understanding of life which is probably partly innate to human beings and partly the product of the practical interaction of human beings and other life forms. Indeed ritual images are constructed on the negation of that understanding. Or, to put the matter in another way, the ritual creates what is merely a paradoxical commentary on processes such as birth, ageing and death, which are familiar to us all, although we might choose to explain their causes differently. The practical perception of these natural processes is the true source of meaning and not the ritual system. Rituals, as we have seen, may attempt to deny this experience of reproduction and the notions of duration on which our understanding of life is grounded but the attempt is always futile since rituals cannot but use at their starting point non-ritual experience. Because of this they can therefore be nothing other than a secondary transformation of that experience.

And ironically the same problem exists for Iteanu. He too, like the rituals he analyses, seeks to deny the ground he stands on, but the enterprise is doomed to failure even before it has started. In spite of his protestations that Orokaiva values only have meanings as defined by the ritual totality, Iteanu has no alternative but to understand and construct that totality for his readers in terms of transformations of what *he* understands by birth, growth, death, exchange, etc. He is justified in doing this, as I have no doubt that the Orokaiva understand these processes much as he does and we do, in terms of our understanding of the experience of growth, reproduction and decay, and not by reference to their total ritual system, since there is growing evidence from cross-cultural psychology that all human beings understand the processes of life and duration in ways which are universal (Atran 1987).

Perhaps the basis of the problem is best revealed in Iteanu's central concept of exchange. He argues that ancestors, spirits, the living and the pigs are all caught up in a roundabout of exchange. As he sees it, in the end all relationships are reciprocal. For example, he sees initiation as the gift of children to the ancestors so that they will give the adults pigs in exchange. In order to build this round to exchange Iteanu uses material from rituals, from practical life and from mythology as though these different phenomena were all of the same kind. This is what enables him to consider the ritual killing of the initiates as the reciprocal equivalent to the immediate and real killing of the pigs and the enemies.

Such idealism, which equates exchange and predation, is surely as unconvincing to the Orokaiva as it is offensive to us. If, however, we are aware that all of us, Orokaiva or readers of this book, are starting from a common base of meaning then we shall see rituals not as aspects of everyday life but as rituals: familiar, constructed, dramatic re-representations of life which attempt to escape an inescapable world. Then we can see that, although symbolic killing may well lead to actual killing, the two are not the same. Similarly, in chapter 7, we shall see that the *as if* speculations of myth cannot be equated either with the experiences of life or the representations of ritual but are rather an intellectual exploration of the lack of fit between the two.

It is because the symbolism of ritual is an attempt to solve problems intrinsic to the human condition and based on a similar understanding of life that ritual systems are so similar and produce such similar political results.

The point of this book is to demonstrate this fundamental identity in a number of ritual systems from varied cultures and to show that this fundamental identity can only be accounted for by the fact that these systems are not internally self-defining but share a common, non-culturally specific base. In so far as this argument convinces, the idealism of Iteanu's position will be disproved.

3

Sacrifice

Chapter 2 began with a discussion of initiation among the Orokaiva. It described how the elders organise a ritual in which the children to be initiated are first associated with pigs, creatures which are seen as very similar to them, and how as pigs the initiates are hunted and symbolically killed by masked men representing ancestral spirits or birds. Then, the initiates are isolated in a dark hut in the forest, where it is said that they, like all those who have gone beyond death, have themselves become a kind of spirit. Finally, the children re-emerge and return from the world of the spirits. They re-emerge associated with the spirits which initially killed them, as hunters and consumers of pigs. However, at this stage the pigs which the initiate will hunt are real pigs. From being conquered and consumed as though they were pigs, the initiates have become conquerors and consumers of pigs and of everything which the pigs evoke: vitality, strength, production, wealth and reproduction.

The initiates' return is accompanied by the whole community, who share in the new-found aggressiveness of the initiates, and all are now predominantly represented as killers of pigs and as eaters of pig meat. As the ritual develops, however, so does the evocation of conquest and soon the killing of pigs is associated with the conquest and killing of people. The pig hunt has come to be a foretaste of warfare and the consumption of enemies.

This matrix of Orokaiva initiation, which is found in many other rituals of initiation, is analogous to the underlying matrix of many of the rituals which have been called sacrifices in anthropological literature. This fundamental connection between sacrifice and initiation has been noted by many commentators. For example Stanner (1960), in a discussion of Australian Aboriginal initiation, shows how the same themes are present there as in biblical sacrifice. Similarly Schwimmer so extends the notion of sacrifice that it includes many aspects of the initiation ritual which was discussed in the previous chapter (1973: 154–9). This continuity will again be argued in this chapter as we compare Orokaiva initiation with a number of rituals which have been called 'sacrifice' by the anthropologists who studied them. In the end, however, this comparison will lead to an even wider comparison of ritual forms, taking in such manifestations as funerary rituals, spirit possession and spirit mediumship.

Although this chapter mainly concentrates on two examples of sacrifice, this is not because sacrifice, any more than initiation, is an easily definable term delimiting a distinct type of ritual. To assume this would almost amount to thinking that every case is a variant of a fundamental and original sacrifice. Like a number of recent writers, such as de Heusch (1986), I believe it is right to stress the great variety that exists among the various examples of 'sacrifice' as they have been described in the literature. A possible reaction to such a complex state of affairs might be to give a restrictive definition of the term, but this would be to take the very opposite strategy to the one I wish to adopt here. Instead, we need not be too concerned about whether a specific ritual is or is not a sacrifice, since the aim of this book is to include all these phenomena within a wider analytical category, which includes considerably more than even the wide range of rituals which have been labelled as sacrifice. Somewhat similarly, de Heusch concludes his book by saying that trance and sacrifice are part of a more general ritual system than is implied by either term. This is convincingly argued, but the ritual system he suggests goes well beyond phenomena which have been called trance and sacrifice and, indeed, goes beyond even what is commonly referred to as religion.

The anthropological concept of sacrifice should, therefore, be treated like the notion of totemism so effectively discussed by Lévi-Strauss (1962). The phenomena which have been called by names such as totemism or sacrifice are not so varied as to make the words useless as general indicators of linked manifestations. On the other hand these manifestations are so loosely connected that it would be as totally pointless to look for an explanation of sacrifice as such as Lévi-Strauss showed it was useless to look for an explanation of totemism as such. Rather, and again like Lévi-Strauss, we must see what are called sacrifices as a few cases of the very many manifestations of a much wider range of phenomena, some of which may have been labelled sacrifices, some initiations, and so on. It is at this more inclusive level that we must seek explanation.

Two examples of sacrifice have been most prominent in the immense non-anthropological literature on the topic, which proliferated especially at the end of the last century. These are ancient Greek sacrifice and biblical sacrifice. A discussion of these familiar cases can therefore serve as an introduction to the approach to be taken in this chapter.

For the ancient Greeks, as for many of the people who have been studied by anthropologists, all meat eating was a sacrifice. The Greeks never killed domestic animals for food for other purposes than sacrifice (Vernant 1979: 44). As in the case of Orokaiva initiation we therefore find an indissoluble link between religion and consumption. Furthermore, the political and military implications of this link are equally present in all these cases. For the Greeks, sacrifices had necessarily to be performed before any legal process could be initiated or before any major act of government could be envisaged. This was because sacrifice gave the sacrificers power and wisdom. Above all, sacrifices were essential before any military enterprise because the performance of the ritual was believed to be strength-giving.

The story of a particularly famous sacrifice has always dominated the traditional nineteenth-century discussions of ancient Greek sacrifice and it can serve to reveal the essential elements of the practice. This is the story of Iphigenia as found in the Greek dramatists, especially the two plays by Euripides, *Iphigenia in Aulis* and *Iphigenia in Tauris*. The Greeks were about to set sail to attack the Trojans when their warlike intentions were weakened by the lack of wind. This problem is normally explained in the Greek sources as a punishment administered by the goddess Artemis for an unspecified offence. A way out of this predicament was, we are told, found in the suggestion made through divination that Agamemnon, the leader of the expedition, should sacrifice his daughter Iphigenia, and thereby launch quite a number of plays and operas. But, in the Euripides version at least, at the very last moment, just as the knife was about to come down, Iphigenia was replaced by a hind, which was killed instead. No doubt this animal would then have been treated like other Greek sacrificial animals. That is, it would be divided into different parts, some of which would be burnt so that the smell could feed the insubstantial gods, while other parts would be roasted and boiled to be consumed by different groups of humans. For humans, unlike the gods who had escaped the transformative cycles of life and death, need the sustaining and strengthening element which comes from consumed flesh (Vernant 1979). Thus fortified, the Greeks got their favourable wind and were ultimately able to kill the Trojans, rape the women, and burn the town.

The overall pattern of the story is strong and clear. Agamemnon, the leader and representative of the Greeks, submits to an attack on himself, or something close to himself: his daughter. For the ancient Greeks, children were thought of as the extension of their fathers. In agreeing, however unwillingly, to carry out the sacrifice, Agamemnon was co-operating with an attack from a god directed against him. The first element of the sequence of sacrificial violence evoked by this story is therefore the partly self-inflicted violence intended by the chief protagonist. But then the violence rebounds and, from having been the victim, Agamemnon becomes a violent actor towards others. He eats the strengthening flesh of the sacrificial animal and not only is he restored bodily, but so is the whole situation and so are all the Greeks; the wind returns, the outward movement of the fleet towards their prey begins and ultimately the process reaches its climax as the Trojans and their town are consumed with fire. From having been conquered Agamemnon has thus become a conqueror.

The other story which is always referred to in the discussions of sacrifice, which appeared in such profusion during the last century, is the biblical story of Abraham and Isaac. According to Genesis, God ordered Abraham to offer his son Isaac in sacrifice instead of the usual sheep. In the end Abraham unwillingly agreed to carry out the divine instructions and began to make the necessary preparations. It is difficult to escape the implication that if the sacrifice had been carried out Isaac would have been killed and perhaps eaten. However, again at the last minute, God substituted a ram and Isaac was spared. Furthermore, as a mark of his favour and in return for obedience and self-denial, God promised Abraham to 'make descendants as many as the stars of heaven and the grains of the sea shore. Your descendants shall gain possession of the gates of their enemies' (Genesis 22: 18).[1]

The similarities between the story of Iphigenia and that of Isaac are very striking and have often been pointed out. Furthermore, the connection between these two stories of sacrifice and the Orokaiva practice of initiation is clear. In all three cases we find the same elements. Firstly, a terrifying closeness to death on the part of the living is evoked. It is as if there was an element of dare in these stories. In the case of Orokaiva initiation the participants stress how very probable it is that the children will not survive the seclusion period of the ritual. In our two sacrifice stories death is avoided by a hair's breadth. Secondly, those who come close to death in all three cases are children, that is members of society who have life before them and who promise social continuation. In other words, the threatened killing is a killing of human vitality at its most intense and forward-looking. The abandonment of this form of vitality would be the abandonment of life itself for the whole community. Thirdly, in all three cases an animal is, at the last moment, substituted for the child. This means that the actual victim's vitality can be completely abandoned in fulfilment of the original promise to God, the gods or the ancestors, who, because of their non-bodily nature, are simply satisfied with receiving the insubstantial aspect of the animal. Fourthly, in all cases the substantial part of the victim, that is its potential vitality, is obtained in the form of meat by the human participants, who thereby replace and regain the vitality which they had lost in the initial self-denial. Fifthly, this consumption enables the whole community to regain vitality and life to such an extent that they can turn their strength outwards in the form of military aggression against other peoples and their children. The spatial aspect of this final, aggressive outward movement is particularly strongly evoked in both of our cases of sacrifice: by the image of the sea journey towards Troy in the one and the biblical reference to the 'gates' of the enemies in the other. Both are images which recall the final military expeditions of Orokaiva initiation.

Several elements of this pattern shared by initiation and sacrifice, especially the movement out of vitality and back again, provided the framework of Hubert and Mauss's 'communication' theory of sacrifice (1968 (1899)). This theory of sacrifice was, until recently, the most widely accepted in anthropology and it was the model for the highly influential study of Nuer sacrifice put forward by Evans-Pritchard (Evans-Pritchard 1956, chapters, 8, 9, 10). It was in this form in particular that Hubert and Mauss's theory came largely to supersede an older theory of sacrifice, which goes back to Plato, where the practice is seen as a matter of obligating the gods by means of a gift.

According to Hubert and Mauss, sacrifice is a matter of going towards the divine via the death of the victim and then coming back to the profane. This may be done for two reasons. Communication may be established through sacrifice in order momentarily to enter into contact with the divine so that sins may be forgiven or other benefits obtained. Hubert and Mauss called these cases 'rites of sacralisation'. Or communication is established with the sacred so that unwanted contact with the supernatural may be brought to an end. These sacrifices were called by the two authors 'rites of desacralisation'. In both cases sacrifice is above all envisaged as the crossing of the barrier between the sacred and the profane (Hubert and Mauss 1968 (1899)).

In spite of the clear advance which Hubert and Mauss's theory represents over previous work, it has recently been fundamentally criticised by a number of writers. The main thrust of that criticism is that Hubert and Mauss were unjustifiably influenced by the prominence they gave to Vedic sacrifice and sacrifice as it is understood in the Judaeo-Christian tradition. This led them to assume that what are in reality quite specific models, derived from particular places and periods, could be used to build a universal theory. Clearly this is an ever-present danger in any attempt to generalise on such a vast subject and the criticism seems particularly well founded in their case, since any theory which uses terms such as 'sacred' and 'profane', terms which cannot be given extracultural referents, cannot form the basis of a general theory of sacrifice or of anything else.[2]

What Hubert and Mauss brought from their reading of ancient Sanskrit texts on sacrifice is the notion that the sacrificer enters the area of the sacred by means of purification of both himself and the victim and can thus communicate with the deity by means of the killing of the victim, which has become a sacred object. For these two authors, sacrifice is a kind of sacrilege which both joins and separates the sacred and the profane. But even if this theory is broadly acceptable for Sanskritic sacrifice – and this will be discussed more fully in the next chapter – it appears that even for ancient India it needs qualification (Biardeau and Malamoud 1976: 19ff.). Even more significantly it is made perfectly clear by writers such as de Heusch, among others, that the idea of a separation between the sacred and the profane in the terms envisaged by Hubert and Mauss is far from universal, and that, in particular, it does not in any way apply to Africa (de Heusch 1986: 20–1).

The unfortunate effect of the Judaeo-Christian heritage on the work is partly inherited from previous writers and partly indulged in anew by Hubert and Mauss. This problem is lucidly identified in an article by the French classicist Detienne, which introduces a number of studies on Greek sacrifice (Detienne 1979). Detienne shows how Hubert and Mauss's work belongs to a long tradition in European history and theology which was already well formulated in the eighteenth century and which reached its apogee in the work of such writers as Cassirer (1972) and Girard (1972). All the writers in this long line implicitly or explicitly sought to make sacrifice the key to the definition of religion and saw Christian ideas of sacrifice as the apogee of lesser forms. As a result they interpreted the phenomena in an evolutionary perspective which saw non-Christian sacrifice as a primitive precursor of the disinterested self-sacrifice of the deity.

Although most of the writers who developed these linked theories were denounced in their time by various orthodox Christians, they were, Detienne convincingly argues, misled by anachronistic or ethnocentric Christian and Jewish concepts. Their work shows, Detienne tells us, 'how an all-encompassing Christianity has continued to exercise a secret and surprising hold on the thought of historians and sociologists who were sure that they were inventing a new science' (1979: 35). This comment has been recently further vindicated by de Heusch's severe examination of how much the famous study of Nuer sacrifice by Evans-Pritchard (1956), which largely follows Hubert and Mauss, has been vitiated by the attempt to translate Nuer concepts into Christian theology and vocabulary (de Heusch 1986: 21–33).

According to Detienne, crypto-Christianity leads to three problems and misrepresentations in the way sacrifice has been viewed both in anthropological literature and beyond. Firstly, he rightly argues that the idea of an evolutionary sequence leading to a higher form of sacrifice has made anthropologists ignore the fact that the various phenomena which they have labelled sacrifice are extremely varied and that they demonstrate no essential unity. Secondly, he argues that the majority of authors have underestimated the political importance of sacrificial practices. Again, this is certainly true though a number of anthropologists and Sanskritists to whom he does not refer, such as Middleton (1960), Luc de Heush (1986), Heesterman (1985) and Gibson (1986), should be acquitted of this charge. Thirdly, Detienne argues that classical anthropologists, with the possible exception of Robertson-Smith, have failed to see the importance of cooking and eating in sacrifice (Robertson-Smith 1889). To make the point Detienne, together with his co-editor Vernant, called their book *Sacrificial Cooking* (1979). In emphasising that aspect of sacrifice they have preceded Gibson (1986), who has stressed the importance of eating and to whose work I shall return. Although this sort of stress is very valuable for our understanding of much apparently obscure ethnography, it becomes even more valuable if we expand Detienne's notion of cooking to a much more general concept than the specifically Greek notions he implies. Indeed, Detienne and Vernant run the risk of being accused of doing precisely what they rightly say Hubert and Mauss did when they universalised Sanskritic ideas, since they themselves appear to attempt to foist Greek ideas on the rest of the world. The idea of the centrality of cooking can, however, be retained if we expand it so that cooking is understood as only one stage in the general transformation of animal food which involves consumption and even digestion (Parry 1985). This process might even be seen to include the escalating chain of consumptions and aggressions, discussed above, which complete rituals of sacrifice and initiation.

I cannot, however, entirely follow Detienne and Vernant when they use their point about cooking as though it negated the significance of the identification of sacrificer and victim and the significance of the self-sacrifice and substitution elements, which so interested Hubert and Mauss, Lienhardt and Evans-Pritchard and which to them are mere crypto-Christianity. The evidence of some form of self-identification, supplied by the authors on whom I rely for the examples discussed in this chapter, seems inescapable though perhaps the general idea needs reformulating. Perhaps this element is absent in the Greek sacrifices which primarily concern Detienne, but we have already seen that the idea was present and central in one story of sacrifice from the same culture, the story of Iphigenia.

It is possible that the reason why Detienne and Vernant do not recognise the centrality of the element of self-identification with the victim in so many forms of sacrifice goes back to a reading of Hubert and Mauss's where their dismissal of the gift theory of sacrifice was a necessary element of and essential preliminary to their own theory. It is true that Hubert and Mauss's dismissal of the gift theory is, as Detienne and Vernant argue, unsatisfactory. The centrality of gift-giving to deities or ancestors in some form is quite inescapable from most cases of sacrifice in the literature. Even in the case of Vedic sacrifice, where quite specific ideas of cosmogony dominate, Biardeau has no hestation in saying that, from the point of view of the sacrificer, the essential act is the giving up of something to the deity (Biardeau and Malamoud 1976: 19). Giving something is the lowest common denominator of rituals which have been called sacrifice, perhaps simply because this is a fundamental meaning of the word in modern European languages. Gift-giving is a central element in the examples discussed by Detienne and Vernant, and ironically it was perhaps their ability to recognise this which led them to reject what Hubert and Mauss have to say so completely, since those authors originally presented their theory as an alternative to gift-theory. This is, however, to pass over much which is of value in Hubert and Mauss's account of sacrifice.

In fact, the importance of gift-giving in sacrifice need not conflict with the idea of self-identification with the victim. We know from Mauss's own work how gifts in very many societies should be seen as part of the giving of the self (1923/4) and Hubert and Mauss again use strikingly similar language to that of the essay on the gift when they stress how inappropriate the contrast between interested and disinterested gift-giving is for the societies to which they are referring (Hubert and Mauss 1968: 305). This means that the giving of an offering closely associated with the self may also be a form of self-identification with the victim and ultimately the recipient. Interestingly, the same point, as it relates to sacrifice, is made by de Heusch when he points out how no sharp boundary can be drawn between being and having in African symbolism (1986: 310–12). In fact the element of consumption and the element of self-sacrifice are both conjointly present in most cases of sacrifice and it is precisely the combination of these two elements which is so revealing. It is this conjunction which makes it possible to demonstrate the relation of sacrifice to initiation and to argue that the symbolic immolation of the almost-self of the first part of sacrifice and the political, military and culinary aspects of the second half mutually imply each other.

To illustrate this point further I shall, by way of illustration, give two ethnographic examples which are in many ways complementary. These are, first, the classic study of the Dinka of the southern Sudan by Lienhardt (1961) and secondly Gibson's recent study of the Buid of the Philippines (1986), which appears to support the position of Detienne and Vernant.

Dinka ethnography is deservedly famous in anthropology and so I shall refer to it only very quickly in order to stress those aspects which are particularly relevant to the general argument. Under normal circumstances Dinka sacrifice centrally involves the killing of cattle. It is these people's most important religious rite and the same would be true of many other African peoples. Most commonly, sacrifices are carried out in time of trouble or when people need strengthening. Very often the immediate cause is disease. This leads us to ask the simple but centrally relevant question: why does killing cattle cure people? But before answering this question we need to begin at the beginning of the sequence of events which culminates in sacrifice as a form of curing.

The initial reason for carrying out the sacrifice is when someone, or a group of people, feels penetrated by an outside force, which is believed either to cause or actually to *be* the disease. Disease is used here in a very wide sense of the word to mean almost any kind of trouble. Lienhardt shows how permeable the Dinka feel to such outside forces and how all trouble is explained in terms of such a bodily invasion.

The next stage in the progression towards sacrifice occurs when the person (or persons) who has been attacked tries to find the cause of the trouble. To do this the patient turns to divination or some other diagnostic procedure and in the process of divination the sequence which leads to sacrifice quickens. What follows the diagnostic is the diviner's recommendation for bringing about a cure and this is particularly revealing. Two apparently totally different and opposed ways of curing are common, especially in Africa. These two ways may be tried concurrently, but more usually they appear as two successive stages of the process of finding a cure, since, if the first is not successful, the other will then be tried. The first way of dealing with intrusion is found universally. Once the source of the trouble has been identified, a way is sought to expel the intrusive force. This way of going about things is familiar to us from western medicine. Indeed the Dinka themselves recognise this identity of form and therefore readily welcome western medicine for this sort of practice.

If this first approach fails, however, then the second tack is tried and that is completely different. In this the diviner will suggest that the disease is a powerful supernatural being, a clan divinity or a spirit for example, which cannot, or should not, be resisted and so, instead of expelling the intrusion, the patient should rather submit to the disease and its attack on her body. She should even draw in and identify with the disease against her body, in other words make her body foreign and accept the intrusion against it. This is not expected to occur without a struggle, but the final victory of the intruding force should not be in doubt.

The lives of Christian saints or the story of Job are well-known examples of this pattern and there are many ethnographic cases of this type of turning round of the person against themselves or rather against the bodily aspect of themselves. For example a particularly fine description of this process is given in the book *Human Spirits* by M. Lambek (1981), where this way of dealing with illness by 'welcome' is shown to lead naturally to spirit possession. After a struggle when the diseased person is still trying out the first tack of expelling the intrusive spirit she finally agrees to the second tack and instead welcomes the spirit. What this means in this case is that she allows her body to be made a receptacle without will, which can be used by an immortal and external spirit for its temporary incarnation (Lambek 1981).

In the case discussed by Lambek this second welcoming approach to disease leads to the instituting of a spirit possession cult, but it could just as easily have been a preliminary to sacrifice. The fact that similar preliminaries can lead to either what we call sacrifice or spirit mediumship shows well how closely these two manifestations are related, a point already made, as we saw, by de Heusch. It also shows once again how misleading the divisions can be within the typology of ritual categories which our academic traditions have imposed. Indeed the close connection between sacrifice and possession can help us understand the Dinka case to which we return.

Here, however, yet another preliminary is necessary before we come to the ritual itself. As was the case for the understanding of Orokaiva initiation, it is necessary to sketch how the Dinka view relations with supernatural beings and with animals, especially cattle. In fact, the main points I want to make on these matters are implicit in the very organisation of Lienhardt's book. The book begins with a discussion of the Dinka's association and near-identification with their cattle. It is made clear that this identification is particularly strong in the case of boys and young men. To illustrate this we are shown a picture of Dinka youth dancing in a way that imitates cattle. The book ends, however, with a discussion of the ritual of the death-defying burial alive of a Dinka priest, the master of the fishing spear. The priest should be a very old man who is buried alive in such a way that, after he has disappeared from sight, nothing but his disembodied voice can be heard singing or speaking an invocation. This complementary opposition between cattle and speech, between the bovine strength of youth and the verbal power of the old, which Lienhardt constructs by the very organisation of the book, is central to Dinka symbolism.

For the Dinka, cattle and humans are very close and this parallelism, which is evocatively discussed by Lienhardt, is familiar from other parts of Africa. This link between cattle and humans is not unlike that which exists between pigs and humans among the Orokaiva. For the Dinka, cattle represent the beauty of strength, vitality and sexuality to which humans aspire, but which they possess in varying amounts. In particular, cattle are associated with young men.

But the similarity between the Orokaiva and Dinka cases goes further. This is because, even though Dinka cattle are seen as similar to humans in some respects, in other, equally significant respects, cattle and humans are very different. These aspects are not so stressed by Lienhardt but they emerge from a careful reading of his ethnography.

For the Dinka, a clear difference between humans and cattle lies in humans' ability to speak. Although Lienhardt does not discuss speech in general, he discusses at great length the speech of the Dinka prophets and of the members of the priestly clan, the masters of the fishing spear. This is a kind of ideal speech, cool speech, not often achieved by less sacred mortals. The Dinka believe that prophets and masters of the fishing spear are the permanent mediums of Divinity and of lesser divinities which, in any case, are simply avatars of the supreme God. The speech of the chosen vessels of Divinity is, therefore, particularly powerful, but it is not exclusive to them. It seems that all men, and perhaps some women, can occasionally make their speech reach similar heights, for example when possessed or when acting as diviners. Perhaps the most important aspect of this quintessential speech is that it is always true. This means that when it is used to talk of the future it is prophetic. Ideally it should be declaimed clearly and require few words (Lienhardt 1961: 139). Everything about this truth-speech contrasts with the associations of cattle. While cattle are youthfully strong but turbulent, mobile, always being exchanged or killed in sacrifice, the true speech of the Dinka is manifested in the old and frail, but is permanent, unchanging, of no particular time and of all times, sober and immortal, beyond process.

This duality of speech and cattle takes many forms. For example the Dinka think of their society as fundamentally divided between warrior clans who are more closely associated with cattle, and priestly clans who bring order, stability and prophetic speech. This kind of distribution suggests an image of complementarity since it implies that both elements are necessary for life. The Dinka see existence as a combination of a bovine animal vitality and a death-defying order crystallised in the invocations of the masters of the fishing spear.

In stressing this duality in Dinka thought I am not doing what Lienhardt rightly warned us against in a recent article on the concept of the self (Lienhardt 1985). There, he very properly stressed how it would misrepresent Dinka thought to argue that they have an explicit theory of what makes up the self. Very sensibly the Dinka say that no one can know what a person is like inside. I believe such justified scepticism is found in most cultures, and I have already tried to stress the dangers of such over-explicit exegesis of ideas of the person in the last chapter. What I am talking about when I say that the Dinka envisage the person as part cattle and part speech is, rather, the dramatic simplifications which are acted out in rituals. In rituals, unlike ordinary, everyday life, an image of the components of interior states is evoked in a way that is partly iconographic and partly allegorical. These dramatic represent-ations are created in order to bring about a symbolic transformation, but they soon fade after the ritual is done, though they never disappear completely.

After the diviner has told the patient that, rather than resist, she must submit to the external invasion, in most cases he will suggest that this is done by sacrificing cattle. Why this is a suitable way of co-operating with the external invader becomes evident in the main actions of the rite. First, the victim is associated with the person for whom the sacrifice is being done. Then, in the first part of the sacrifice proper the animal is threatened for long periods with the spear of the sacrificer and it is weakened in a variety of ways but principally by exposure to the sun. Ultimately it is killed. But simultaneously, as this is happening, the other aspect of human society, the cold speech of truth, is strengthened and conquers. Speech is manifest in sacrifice in the invocations and prayers spoken by the master of the fishing spear which dominate the first part of the ritual. The Dinka say that it is the continual speaking of these invocations which weakens and kills the animal and makes its horns, prime symbols of vitality and virile strength, wilt and droop. The very word which the Dinka use as a verb for 'to invoke' suggests the violence that is being done to the sacrificial animal as it can also mean 'to attack an enemy' (1961: 263). The drama is a tilting of the balance between vitality and unchanging truth, in which vitality is vanquished.

It is, therefore, right to see Dinka sacrifice as involving an identification between sacrificer and victim, as Lienhardt does in the case of the Dinka and as Evans-Pritchard for the Nuer. In spite of de Heusch's objections much of the ethnography confirms their point of view. However, the proposition has to be qualified since it is only *one* aspect of the sacrificer and the community, the vital cattle aspect, which is symbolically weakened and killed in the ritual, but the other aspect, the speech aspect, is strengthened at the very same time as vitality ebbs away. This is why theories of the identification of sacrificer and victim have often been criticised but never overcome. It is not the whole person, which is identified with the victim, but only one aspect.

Dinka sacrifice is in its first part a drama of conflict between cattle and speech; as the animal is defeated speech and invocation become triumphant. What the ritual creates by evocation is first a reduction of the complexity of the person and society so that it can appear to consist merely of two opposed elements, the cattle and the invocation, which are represented as visually and auditorily in conflict. Once the image has been established the ritual can reach the next stage as, finally, the speech element conquers.

For the sacrificer and the community the conquest and the killing of the cattle is an external drama which can be experienced as corresponding to the weakening and killing of the cattle element by now evoked in the body. It is in this ritual context, and this context only, that is right to speak of elements of the person because, in the ritual, different external entities are brought into action to represent and create an internal conflict. What is happening is similar to a morality play where the struggle of good and evil within a protagonist can be represented as objectified by different actors.

But ritual is more complex and more powerful than this simple comparison suggests. Firstly, as will be discussed below, the second half of the ritual breaks away from the theatrical model. Secondly, even in the first part of the ritual discussed above, we are not just dealing with an externalised representation of an internal state, but also with actions which have an experienced internal effect on the body of the participants.

The drama of the victory of speech over cattle occurs out in the open on the ceremonial ground. But the same division and the same tipping of the balance also occurs experientially for both the sacrificer and for those less centrally concerned. In order to understand how the killing of the cattle is bringing about a cure it is better to concentrate on this aspect first.

The effect of the ritual on the peripheral participants is revealing in many ways. First, it shows how, in a ritual such as this and in a society such as that of the Dinka, the boundary between the body of an individual and the wider group is weak (Bloch 1988). Thus, in the Dinka ritual of sacrifice, as in Orokaiva initiation, even though the event might be focused on the central actor (the initiate or the patient), all the others present are not onlookers but co-participants. This continuity manifests itself at the point in the ritual when, as the animal on the ritual ground is weakened and as the speech side is magnified, the onlookers also experience speech overwhelming their internal vitality and they become possessed and speak the words of Divinity. Lienhardt gives a graphic description of the twitching of the flesh of the possessed young men, their cattle side, as it submits to the verbal invasion of Divinity. This twitching of the flesh of the possessed serves well to show how a parallel has been established between the external visible actions of the participants in the ritual and the invisible experiential process which goes on inside their bodies, since the Dinka themselves stress the identity of this twitching of the flesh of the possessed participants with the twitching of the flesh of the animal as it is being slaughtered (1961: 137).[3]

The falling into trance of some of the onlookers is illuminating in a number of ways. First, we have once again demonstrated the close affinity of sacrifice and spirit possession. Secondly, because spirit possession is a matter of the triumphant penetration of a transcendental being into the conquered body of a medium, we can see that this is also what sacrifice is all about, that, like spirit possession, it is an appropriate response to the diviner's advice not to resist disease, but rather join the invader entering into your body. In the ritual the sacrificial animal is made to stand for the vitality of the body of the sacrificer while the transcendental speech of the invocations of the master of the fishing spear appropriately represents and is a manifestation of Divinity. By organising the sacrifice the patient is thus completing the attack on his own vitality in order to let the permanent triumph. The weakening and death of the animal is the culmination of this process and publicly represents the victory of transcendental speech. The first part of sacrifice and possession is the completion of the process of joining the invader against one's vital self.

And, of course, all this is exactly what happens in a ritual such as Orokaiva initiation, or rather in the first part of the ritual when the pig element in the children is weakened and killed so that the spiritual element can dominate. But then, with sacrifice as with initiation, there is a reversal. The abandonment of strength and vitality cannot be final. As with initiation, it must be regained. The internal lack of balance in the body, brought about by the victory of the transcendental, must be redressed if life is to go on. And again this poses the problem of how to avoid contradiction so that the second part of sacrifice is not merely a reincorporation of what has so painfully been got rid of.

The Dinka sacrifice solution is very similar to the Orokaiva initiation solution and it revolves around the change in the relation of the sacrificer and victim which occurs at the moment of the actual killing. Lienhardt, like other ethnographers, notes how a dramatic transformation in mood occurs at this point. This is due to the fact that the close association of sacrificer and victim ends at this moment. Up to then there has been a painfully close experiential analogic relation between the two, but once the killing has been done the sacrificer is freed and the dead animal is merely a dead animal on the ground, ready to be cut up and eaten in the second part of the ritual. When that occurs the relation of the victim, on the one hand, and the sacrificer and community, on the other, changes from the analogic to the physical, just as, among the Orokaiva, the pigs of the first part of the initiation were metaphoric pigs while the pigs of the second half are real pigs.

From this point on Lienhardt almost seems to lose interest in the proceedings for reasons which have much to do with his highly intellectual definition of religious experience, which seems to have no place for what is fundamentally a feast. In this point of view he reflects the approach of those writers whom Detienne rightly criticises for crypto-Christianity and for ignoring the political and consumption aspects of sacrifice in spite of the fact that these aspects are just as present in Christianity. However, if we again agree with Detienne on this, it is not say that what interested Lienhardt is not equally important.

What happens in the second part of the ritual is that the animal is cut up, distributed and partly eaten there and then amidst a good deal of celebration. By this stage this meat has taken on a quite different meaning from what it had in the first part. No longer does it represent the animal, vital side of the sacrificer; it has become, by the simple fact of killing, the meat of an animal which, because it is an animal, is by nature alien to humans. Its vitality can be consumed without problem by those present in order that, like all meat, it will restrengthen them through its nutritive value.

Unlike Lienhardt, and even more Evans-Pritchard writing of the nearby Nuer, the Dinka attach very great importance to the feast side of sacrifice and to the eating of cattle, in which they revel. Indeed, the Dinka word which Lienhardt translates as 'sacrifice' would, according to him, be more straight-forwardly translated as 'feast', thereby making a nonsense of the refusal to consider the meal as part of the sacrifice (1961: 281). The eating of the meat of the cattle restores vitality which had been analogically lost in the first part of the ritual. Those who had allowed their native vitality to be symbolically vanquished by following the advice of the diviner and performing the sacrifice are now rewarded with the actual vitality of an external being. The meal is that highly pleasurable recovery of this vitality, which has been surrendered in the first part of the proceedings. And here, as with the other consumptions which follow rebounding conquests, this may not be just a restoration of lost vitality. The recovery is triumphalist and outwardly directed. It may indeed lead to a legitimate increase in vitality since the vitality that is now being recovered is conquered and ordered by the transcendental order of the speech of the masters of the fishing spear.

By having allowed one side of themselves to die so that they may become pure speech the Dinka sacrificers can regain the cattle side through the mouth, almost exactly as happened for the Orokaiva initiate. There is a difference in the two cases but it is slight. In the case of Orokaiva initiation it was the children who were representing pigs in the first part of the proceedings, while in the first part of Dinka sacrifice it is the cattle which represents the humans, but this difference is of no significance to the general logic of the proceedings.

And the parallel between the two rituals does not end there. For the Orokaiva the consumption of the external pig was also the promise of further more adventurous conquests of a political and military form and, again, the same is true of the Dinka. As in the case of the Orokaiva, Dinka sacrifice takes on a more military idiom as it proceeds. Lienhardt tells us that to 'make a feast or sacrifice often implies war' (1961: 281), indeed that the rituals often ended either in threatened or real military raids. The expansionist reconquest of vitality is shown once again to lead either to restoration, as in the return of the initiates to the village, or to aggrandisement.

It is because the sacrifice ends in such a feast, which involves not just the legitimate recovery of vitality but, by extension, the recovery of more vitality, as much as one can get, that sacrifice can cure disease in all its forms whether physical or, as is often the case, social and moral. What has happened in the sacrifice is that the specific problem, which was the original cause of the ritual, has been dealt with in a way which is not specifically addressed to it but is, rather, an action which generally reactivates the strength and activity of the social group and which, it is hoped, will overcome the particular difficulty with its general force. This is why the same rituals can be used both to cure specific ills and on a non-specific basis to reactivate the right order of man in society and nature, such as occurs, for example, in annual fertility rituals such as the famous Ncwala of the Swazi (Beidelman 1966). This point will be discussed further in the next chapter. However, because the culinary, political and military sides are not developed by Lienhardt, it is best to turn to other ethnographies to understand the second half of sacrifice.

The second ethnographic example to be considered in any detail in this chapter is a recent study of the Buid of Mindoro in the Philippines by Gibson (1986). In many ways this ethnography of sacrifice is almost the opposite of that on the Dinka and, as a result, it complements it admirably for the purposes of the present argument. Gibson insists that, while the element of substitution of the sacrificer for the victim is central to the Dinka, it is absent in Buid sacrifice. On the other hand, he argues that the communal and politically significant strength-giving meal in which the animal is eaten is the most important aspect of Buid sacrifice. This approach would certainly delight Detienne. The differences have as much to do with the different approaches of the two authors as they have to do with differences between Africa and South East Asia. However, in spite of the wide cultural differences, it is to a certain extent possible to reconcile the two studies.

We must start by a consideration of Buid notions of the person as they emerge in ritual. Gibson tells us that the Buid consider that the person is made up of three elements. These three elements he glosses as body, mind and soul. The body and soul are acquired through the biological processes of birth. They are closely linked. Gibson tells us that the state of the body reflects the state of the soul (1986: 126), but the soul, unlike the body, does not disappear at death but becomes a ghost. Both the soul and the body are driven by asocial, individualistic desires, such as the desire for food and exclusive sexual gratification. These desires are normally controlled by the third element, the mind. The mind develops with adulthood, begins to weaken with the onset of senility and finally disappears at the death of an individual. The manifestation of the mind can be seen in the self-control exercised by the person and by their socially co-operative attitude. The faculty of speech is a sign of the mind and this is especially so in the highest form of speech, the chanting of the spirit mediums. In these concepts the Buid are surprisingly close to the Dinka and this similarity is increased when we take into account Buid ideas about the relation of humans and pigs, ideas which are reminiscent of Dinka ideas about the relation of humans and cattle.

For the Buid, animals share with humans the body and the soul, both of which are driven by desires, but, as might be expected, it is the controlling mind, and therefore speech, which is the element that differentiates humans, especially Buid humans, from animals. The negative side of animality should, however, be balanced with the positive aspect of animality, which is its vitality. Indeed, it appears that, because their bodies and souls are not under the control of mind, the Buid feel that the vitality of animals is somehow stronger than that of humans.[4] From Gibson's book one gets the feeling of a considerable amount of anxiety about the possible lack of differentiation between humans and animals, especially pigs, since pigs are, as he points out, very close to humans because they are domesticated and live directly under the house (1986: 153–5).[5] The Buid seem to be saying that, but for the control of the mind, humans would be like pigs and their society would be as chaotic as that of pigs, as each and every individual would seek to fulfil their selfish desires.

Furthermore, this partial identity with pigs means that, if humans were not under the control of the mind, they would, like pigs who are eaten by humans, become legitimate food for superior beings. How real this worry is becomes clear in the context of funerals, where it is believed that because the dead have lost the protection of their minds and are therefore like pigs, they immediately become potential prey to pig-eating spirits, who treat the corpse as though it were pork. In certain contexts the Buid say that 'they are the pigs of the spirits' (1986: 150). One might see this statement as being a shorthand for saying that, but for the protection of the mind, they are as vulnerable to flesh-seeking spirits as pigs are to humans.

The way the mind offers protection from pig-eating spirits is clearest in the rituals of spirit mediumship which are central to Buid religion. Buid spirit mediumship is, like all aspects of Buid society, strikingly democratic, or rather, corporatist. Nearly all households contain a person who, by means of a secret chant, can summon at least one spirit familiar who will make mediumship possible. The summoning of these familiars is so common that Gibson tells us it is very rare for a night to go by in a settlement without some medium being heard chanting. The summoning of familiars by chanting has the purpose of enabling the mind to soar 'on the back' of the familiar above the settlement. The reason for such acts of mediumship is, above all, to protect the community from various malevolent spirits who are always seeking to attack the souls of the members as a preliminary to being able to eat their bodies after death.

This almost daily guard-duty is achieved by the process, already much discussed in this book, whereby animal-like vitality is abandoned by the mediums. As a result of chanting, the mind of the medium separates from their soul and body and the freed mind begins to be able to see the medium's familiar approaching. The mind then gets on the back of the familiar and, as it soars, it leaves behind on the ground the merely animal sides of the person, that is the body and the soul.

Again, as in the examples discussed in the earlier parts of this book, this abandonment of vitality is like what happens after death, since the Buid believe that after death the mind returns to a transcendental, undifferentiated community of minds and only the body and the soul remain on earth for a while. The body is then eaten by the evil predatory spirits and the soul becomes for a limited period an egoistical ghost.

The similarity of this example with those from the Dinka or the Orokaiva cases is far from total. In the Buid example the transcendental element, the mind, does not survive the death of the person and is thus different from the

Orokaiva spirit aspect which becomes an immortal ancestral spirit. The contrast is further heightened by the fact that the element which *does* survive after death, that is the soul, shares in the animality of the body. These differences are, however, less significant than might at first appear.

This becomes apparent as we return to the subject of Buid mediumship. The almost nightly chanting sessions, which normally involve only one medium, are actually best understood as minor preparations, or practice sessions, for much more elaborate Buid rituals, which Gibson calls seances. These seances are usually occasioned by some major trouble or disease. What makes them different from more common acts of mediumship is the co-operation of a large number of mediums and the presence of the whole community. The point of these large gatherings is that the various mediums can join forces and drive away the powerful evil spirits, who have succeeded in invading the community in spite of the vigilance of the lone medium's nightly patrol. Gibson is at his most evocative when he describes how seances are joint enterprises manifesting the ethos of sharing and solidarity, which the Buid value above all and which is the product of the control exercised by the minds of all the mediums of the community working together.

In such seances the minds of all the important men and some women, helped by their many familiars, are joined together to defeat the intruders. This powerful image of intellectual co-operation enables us to understand better that what Gibson calls the 'mind' is not primarily an individual part of the person, but an aspect of a holistic appreciation of the local society. Indeed, such a view of the mind as that which leads to sharing accords well with the general conclusions of Gibson's book. In the seance it is the minds of the community together with their familiars which are once again gathered to fight against the unending intrusions of the spirits. This community of minds and familiars is therefore transcendental to the individual mind of any one person.

By continuing to share the powers of their minds and familiars the Buid act, not as individuals, but as a community. Also, as a community, they are making a bid for survival after individual death. There is, therefore, a sense in which the community of minds and familiars is immortal since, although the minds of individuals come and go, the corporate body of minds remains. This is even clearer in the case of the spirit familiars since these, unlike anything else in Buid society, are inherited by one person from another, thereby implying the familiars' separation from human mortality. This community of minds and spirits is the permanent element of Buid society; it corresponds to the speech of the masters of the fishing spear and the ancestors of the Orokaiva. All these transcendental elements are opposed to individual and unstable elements associated with animals and their vitality, an element which is represented, in the Buid case, by the body and the selfish soul.

If this argument is accepted we are some way towards showing the close parallel which exists between Lienhardt's study of Dinka sacrifice, which stresses the identification of victim and sacrificer, and Gibson's study of Buid sacrifice, which stresses the importance of killing the animal, cooking and eating it. First, however, we must look more closely at precisely these elements in Buid ethnography.

The important seances of the Buid, when the whole community gets together, not only involve spirit mediumship, but also what Gibson calls sacrifices, that is the ritual killing, cooking and eating of an animal: a pig or a chicken. These sacrifices are carried out for a number of different reasons. Here, for lack of space, I shall concentrate only on the two most different cases: when the spirits concerned in the sacrifice are beneficial to humans and when the spirits are totally hostile to humans.

Gibson gives an example of a case of the latter type, which was necessitated when a child was believed to be diseased because his house had been invaded by a whole horde of harmful spirits. In order to deal with this trouble a large seance was organised involving many spirits and many mediums. As people began to gather, the spirit mediums called their familiars by chanting, then they began to co-ordinate their various visions into a shared one. It was during this time that what Gibson calls the sacrifice took place. The participants hung a pig upside down from the rafters and then swung it over the child's head. Just as they slaughtered the animal the mediums urged the spirits to leave the child.

Although Gibson would disagree, I think it is inevitable that we must see the killing of the pig as a substitute for the child, which the evil spirits had begun to attack by biting, a form of aggression which the Buid see as a preliminary to aggressive eating. But then, as in Dinka sacrifice, after the moment of the slaughter, everything changes. The insubstantial spirits have been fed the insubstantial soul of the pig and so the humans can indulge as a community in a revivifying meat feast which is specially intended to strengthen the stricken child (Gibson 1986: 158–9).[6]

When the sacrifice is intended to bring about the intervention of beneficial spirits the ritual is a little different. In the case discussed by Gibson (1986: 172–9) the intent is to bring back the presence of those beneficial spirits who had withdrawn because of an antisocial act by some members of the community. As always, the Buid first try to contact the spirits through the double intermediary of the mediums and their familiars and, as they do this, they invitingly kill the pig on the threshold. They then proceed to the equally important revivifying feast, which, as Gibson convincingly demonstrates, expresses and reinforces the idiom of sharing on which Buid society rests. In the case of the sacrifice to beneficial spirits, and as when evil spirits are addressed, the spirits are invited to come and share in the communal meal. Because of this the spirits are given a little bit of meat to evoke their presence in the human group and enable them to join in.

It is the very great importance which the Buid attach to these feasts, which makes Gibson take a general view of sacrifice which conflicts with that of such writers as Lienhardt and Evans-Pritchard. He argues, as Robertson-Smith did, that Buid sacrifice is only focused on the element of a uniting communal meal and that it lacks the element of self-sacrifice and substitution which was central for Hubert and Mauss and Evans-Pritchard. In this conclusion he joins Detienne although, as far as I know, the two authors wrote quite independently of each other.

The way I see the matter is somewhat different from any of these authors. Gibson's conclusion would follow if one used the label 'sacrifice' as though it denoted a discrete analytical category defined by a concern with the ritual killing and consumption of an animal. There is no doubt that this is how the word has been used in the anthropological literature. If one limits the analysis of Buid sacrifice to acts defined in this way, the conclusion reached by Gibson that Buid sacrifice is only a matter of eating the victim is largely convincing, even though the element of substitution is not, even on his own evidence, absent.[7]

But if, like de Heusch, Detienne and myself, we assume that sacrifice cannot be defined cross-culturally and that the word is nothing more than a pointer to a cluster of phenomena which are contained within a wider family of rituals, there is no reason why we should limit our explanatory attempt to the pig killing and eating and ignore other parts of the seance. Indeed, there is a good reason why we should not do so since the Buid themselves make no such distinction. It therefore seems reasonable to analyse the event as a totality, containing both the element of spirit mediumship and the element of pig killing.

If we do this we find that Buid ritual practice becomes much closer in structure to Dinka sacrifice and that it accords with the general pattern of rebounding violence discussed in this book. Buid spirit mediumship is a response to a form of potential trouble, which is imagined as an invasion of hostile invisible forces. The response to such invasion is not to identify with the invading forces, as would be the case in Orokaiva initiation or in Dinka sacrifice, and then turn against one's vitality, but it is something not all that dissimilar. Although the Buid do not join with the invading spirits they transform their society into something of the same order as that of the spirits, a community of insubstantial minds and familiars. In doing this they anticipate individual death since, as will happen after death, they abandon their vital, animal-like element, that is their souls and bodies. But, just as they individually die a little, they are also reconstituted into a wider, non-individual and life-transcending unity, which endures through time as people come and go.

Thus, the part of the seance concerned with spirit mediumship corresponds fairly closely to the first part of Dinka sacrifice with its abandonment of animal vitality in favour of the eternal and unchanging truth of the speech entrusted in the clan of the masters of the fishing spear. In both cases we have an abandonment of practical dialectics which is achieved by a self-inflicted conquest of one side of the self, though in one case this is achieved through the drama of Dinka spirit possession and, in the other, by the extreme control implied in Buid mediumship.

But, as in the other cases we have looked at, this movement to the permanent transcendental cannot be maintained for ever if life is to go on and vitality to be regained, though, as in the other cases, since vitality cannot be regained in the form in which it was lost, it must be regained from an alien source. And so the part of the seance not concerned with mediumship is concerned with what Gibson has called 'sacrifice' and eating. Since the mediums cannot remain in their transcendental state and the community cannot be left hanging in mid air they must, like the Dinka in the second part of sacrifice, regain vitality and therefore mortality, which they do through the shared consumption of pig meat.

In the case of a large-scale seance the Buid think of both the departure to the spirit world and the return to vitality as communal matters and it is therefore particularly appropriate that one of the central aspects of the rebounding violence of external vitality among the Buid takes the form of a 'communal' meal which incarnates that central Buid value, the idiom of sharing.

Gibson, better than any other ethnographer, shows the significance of the meat eating and how its meaning is to be found just as much in the physiological responses it evokes as in more intellectual associations. This, I am sure, would also have been the case for the Dinka had Lienhardt chosen to include that part of the proceeding in his analysis of sacrifice.

In other words it is the totality of the various types of Buid seances, which all share the same two critical elements – spirit mediumship and meal – which is a close equivalent to the whole of Dinka sacrifice, involving as it does both invocation and feast. It is only Gibson's and Lienhardt's different definition of the event which has led to their appearing to reach such contrasting positions. And, furthermore, both cases are very similar to the Greek and Jewish examples of sacrifice with which this chapter began.

These four cases of sacrifice reveal themselves to be also fundamentally similar to Orokaiva initiation in that all these rituals are based on the same sequence. Firstly, there is a representation of a bifurcation of life between an exaggeratedly chaotic vitality and a transcendental, permanent order which is the basis for institutions. Secondly, there is a representation of the abandonment of chaotic vitality, an abandonment which is caused by an attack on the vital chaotic aspect of the self or of the community. Thirdly, we have a triumphalist recovery of mastered and consumed vitality obtained from an external source.

There is an aspect of the Buid ethnography which, however, seems to go against the assimilation of this case to examples from Dinka or Orokaiva ethnography. One aspect of these ethnographies, emphasised in what has gone before, is how the experience of reproduction becomes the basis for an ideological transformation which I have called rebounding violence and which creates an idiom and a legitimation for aggression and military expansionism. But military expansionism and aggression are, as Gibson clearly shows, values which are totally alien to the Buid, a people who have a horror of all forms of aggression and who will not engage in any kind of domination which would imply the superiority of one person over another. The cause of this lack of aggressiveness is found by Gibson in Buid history. The Buid have for many centuries been in permanent retreat from external aggressors infinitely more powerful than themselves. Their strategy for dealing with this situation has been to withdraw from contact with outsiders and to emphasise egalitarian sharing amongst themselves. The Buid know that any kind of aggression on their part is not possible and, indeed, that it would be counterproductive. So, unlike the Dinka or the Orokaiva, they use the symbolism of rebounding violence to achieve reproduction and that is all. They conquer their pigs like the Orokaiva, but, unlike the Orokaiva, this conquest is not the preliminary for further and different conquests.

That, however, is not to say that the symbolism which underlies Buid religious practice does not contain within itself the possibility of being transformed into an aggressive variant. Indeed, the ethnography of the Philippines offers us proof of this. In two striking books M. and R. Rosaldo unravelled much of the symbolism of the Ilongot peoples of central Luzon (M. Rosaldo 1980; R. Rosaldo 1980). Anyone reading their work side by side with Gibson's study cannot but be struck by how similar the basic religious concepts of the Buid and the Ilongot actually are. And yet, in total contrast to the Buid, the Ilongot are a people who value aggression and especially anger, anger which ultimately manifests itself in headhunting directed fairly indiscriminately outside the basic social group.

The similarity and the difference are instructive. The cause of the difference is the different situations in which the Buid and the Ilongot have found themselves during history. Unlike the Buid, the Ilongot were left relatively in peace and had a number of opportunities to attempt to expand. In those conditions the same basic symbolic and religious elements developed in a totally different, aggressive direction.

This comparison can perhaps help us to begin to specify the relation of the idiom of rebounding violence to the reality of military aggression and of actual political forms. The basis of the symbolism is the need for establishing apparently immortal human structures on the necessarily mobile base of human reproduction. This is done by creating an image of an inverted reproduction which ultimately requires the symbolic or actual presence of outsiders, who are there to have their vitality conquered, but who, unlike the main participants, do not then go on to conquer. This construction contains within itself the possibility of a further transformation into an imperialistic form, which appears to flow imperceptibly from the requirements of symbolic reproduction. Whether that potential of the symbolism will be developed and exploited cannot, however, be explained by an analysis of the symbolism itself. This depends on the real circumstances – political, economic and military circumstances – in which people find themselves. When the actors of the ideology of rebounding conquest are weak and in retreat they will, like the Buid, develop the potential of the structure so that it is only concerned with reproduction. Then the image of consumption of vitality and aggression will stop at the animals. But in different historical circumstances, when expansionist aggression is a real possibility, as it sometimes was for the Ilongot, the symbolism of the reconsumption of vitality is expanded and it becomes a legitimation of outwardly directed aggression.

4

Cosmogony and the state

The two previous chapters examined single rituals apparently carried out for specific purposes: the Orokaiva ritual was carried out in order to initiate a group of children; the Dinka sacrifices I discussed were intended to overcome specific problems; Buid spirit mediumship and sacrifice were concerned with defeating or encouraging spirits. However, in each case the analysis moved away by almost imperceptible degrees from the instrumental aspect to a general discussion of the processes which these rituals represent as animating society. This slippage actually reflects the way the rituals operate; in all three cases the rituals dissolve the particular purpose into a general idiom of societal regeneration.

In his book Iteanu is rightly insistent that the Orokaiva initiation ritual is only one part of a wider interconnected ritual system which includes mortuary rituals and marriage rituals (Iteanu 1983). Even more revealing is the way the initial movement ot the initiates from the village to the seclusion hut in the bush and back again is envisaged as being only a part of a general oscillation between these two locations. This back-and-forth movement involves all adult members of society throughout their lives and can also be imagined as involving the dead, who regularly reinvade the village as masked spirits, later returning to the bush to begin the process again at the next ritual. Orokaiva initiation ritual is revealed as part of a general image of an ordering movement, both cyclical and creative, which involves all society for all time regardless of particular actors or the particular stages in which their lives are implicated.

Similarly, even though most Dinka sacrifices are concerned with specific ends, the rituals evoke a similar general image of the construction of the world in controlled but dynamic form, where the permanent austere morality of the masters of the fishing spear frames and organises, but is also animated by, the vitality of cattle. This is what explains the fact that in societies such as the Dinka the ritual of sacrifice can serve so many different purposes: curing, marking rites of passage, or, indeed, no specific purpose at all, as in annual regenerative rituals. Thus we find that the Dinka, on occasions which should occur every seven years, carry out general unspecific tribe-wide sacrifices which regenerate and re-enact the general order of society, and that these totalising rituals follow exactly the same general lines as sacrifices intended to bring about specific cures.

This merging of the specific with the general is best known in the anthropological literature from the case of Vedic and classical Indian sacrifice. Indian sacrifice was of course Hubert and Mauss's central example, but a vast literature has grown up on the subject. One point which is continually stressed by commentators, especially Sanskritists, is how every act of sacrifice refers back to an all-encompassing image of the creation of the world (Biardeau and Malamoud 1976). Vedic sacrifice, Heesterman tells us, is 'a periodic quickening ritual by which the universe is recreated' (Heesterman 1959: 245–6, quoted in Parry 1982: 77). The idea of a particular ritual being merely an aspect of a much wider process is probably pushed even further in Indian sacrifice than in the Orokaiva or Dinka case where only the idea of regenerating a particular social group within a particular territory is evoked. The principle is the same, however, and so it seems appropriate to use the term cosmogonic, which is normally applied to Hindu sacrifice, for all the examples touched on so far in order to stress how all these rituals dissolve the specific into a general process re-enacting the creation of moral life.

The Indian material most directly comparable with previous chapters is probably anthropological studies of Hindu sacrifice. These studies show that the general principle of rebounding violence applies in the same way to rituals which, as the actors are consciously aware, are part of an all-encompassing system as it does to the apparently more limited ritual phenomena so far considered. A brief consideration of the significance of the cosmogonic aspects of Hindu sacrifice can therefore serve as a bridge between the first part of the book, which examines particular rituals, and the second part, which will mainly concentrate on total systems.

A number of writers concerned with Hinduism have argued that the model of cosmogonic sacrifice organises and unites all Hindu religious phenomena (Biardeau and Malamoud 1976) and the way Hindu concepts of sacrifice can, in this way, link the specific with the macrocosmic is well illustrated by a number of studies by J. Parry devoted to funeral practices in the holy Indian city of Benares (Parry 1981, 1982).

The town of Benares is associated with the two principal gods of the modern Hindu pantheon. The city is dedicated to Siva who dominates. He is, in Benares at least, primarily associated with renunciation and asceticism. But Benares also contains the place where the kingly Vishnu is believed to have created the world. This place is a burning *Ghat* on the shore of the Ganges where numerous Hindus come to die, to take the ashes of relatives and, above all, to have bodies cremated.

The reason why the place where the world was created is an appropriate funeral ground is linked to the fact that Hindus can conceive of the cremation of the corpse as an act of sacrifice in which the body is a sacrificial offering given by the dead person (Parry 1981, 1982). In this perspective the corpse is seen as still animate until the actual cremation. This means that in coming to Benares to be cremated, either on her own initiative or *post mortem* with the help of relatives and friends, the dying person is willingly offering her body to the gods. In this way cremation therefore becomes a final act of ascetic renunciation.

This aspect of Hindu funerals and sacrifice can be seen as yet another example of the first part of rebounding violence: a willing co-operation by the subject, in this case the dying person, with a transcendental attack and penetration of her vitality. And again, as in the other examples, this attack on the native vitality of the subject implies a violent recovery of vitality from an external source.

This recovery of vitality might be somewhat unexpected in a funerary context. After all, in the earlier examples discussed the first part of rebounding violence was modelled on funerals, while the second part of the rituals abandoned this symbolism to replace it with that of military conquest, or cooking and eating, or even hunting. It might be assumed that in the case of actual funerals this second half would not occur. This is not so for two reasons. First of all the dead may be believed to re-enter the vital world in some form or other. Thus the Orokaiva spirits reconquer the youth of the village at every initiation. Secondly, in all societies which are not totally dominated by an individualist ideology, the death of a person is seen as merely an event in a greater, more inclusive continuity involving other members of the community. Parry shows how both elements are present in the funerary practices in Benares.

Parry is mainly concerned to show how, in spite of the general renunciation elements of the actual cremation, the post-cremation rituals are concerned in various ways with a recreation of the body of the dead. Thus a series of rice balls, called by the same word as for a human embryo, serve to represent the recreation of the body of the dead person. One of these, when eaten by mourners, can be seen as a kind of semen fertilising barren women (Parry 1982: 84–6). Similarly the austerities performed by the chief mourner after the death are said to give him ultimately 'the power to recreate the body of the deceased' (Parry 1982: 86).

In spite of these clear elements of regeneration, if this was all there was to the matter, we would only be seeing a very weak shadow of the triumphalist and aggressive aspects of the manifestations of rebounding conquest which have appeared in the examples considered so far. These aspects emerge, however, much more clearly when we consider the homology between funerals and the creative sacrifice of Vishnu which every funeral re-enacts.

Vishnu is believed to have carried out prolonged austerities on the very site of the Benares cremation *Ghat* to which the bodies of the dead are taken. These austerities on the part of the god are believed to have led to the creation of the world. The reason for this, Parry tells us, following O'Flaherty, is that the ascetic attack on one's own vitality paradoxically induces creative heat which both consumes and fertilises. It is this process which cremation re-enacts. The dying person, by willingly immolating herself on the funeral pyre, is repeating Vishnu's act of creation. In both cases the process begins with an attack on native vitality which leads to fire which leads to creation, or rather recreation (Parry 1982: 77).

This combination of asceticism and of the creation of earthly vitality takes us back to the two principal deities of Benares: Siva and Vishnu. Siva, in Benares at least, predominantly represents the ascetic aspects of the halting of vitality. The presence of Siva is continually evoked by the necrophagous ascetics who roam the *Ghats* and are Siva's devotees (Parry 1982). This ascetic aspect is also present in the funeral itself in the element of willing self-immolation which should be the prelude to cremation. Vishnu, by contrast, is associated with the life-giving practice of sacrifice itself, which in the funeral takes the form of the actual cremation.

The contrast between those two aspects of the ritual and the two Benares representations of the deities is, however, marked by only a fine and unstable dividing line. This is shown by that fact that each deity implies the other and that both are sometimes believed to be manifestations of the same supreme god (Biardeau 1972: 136–8). Furthermore, even when separated, the two deities can each represent something of the other. Siva is often symbolised by an erect phallus, which can stand both for arrested reproduction (asceticism) and for reproduction itself, which is the very opposite of asceticism. Indeed, this possibility is developed in the South Indian cults of the consorts of Siva (Fuller 1984: 6–10). Similarly, Vishnu may be a violent sacrificial creator, but he only achieves this status after a long period of Siva-like asceticism.

This linking up of the opposed deities can be easily understood in the context of a sacrificial ritual such as cremation. The asceticism of the renunciation of the body is represented as ideally leading seamlessly to the sacrificial Vishnuite phase of cremation. Because of this concluding association with Vishnu the corpse is therefore also seen as a recreator of vitality.

However, this association with Vishnu has yet other implications. It is these further implications which bring the element of aggressive consumption to this Hindu example. In Hinduism, Vishnu is seen as both the ideal sacrificer and the ideal king; indeed the two roles are represented as mutually implying each other (Biardeau 1972: 75). It is the royal element which completes the parallel between this case and the other examples in this book.

The Hindu idiom of kingship implies exactly that image of the consuming conqueror evoked in the final part of the rituals examined in the previous chapters. In much Sanskritic literature the king is represented as the legitimate vanquisher of his subjects; he is said to be their 'eater' (Heesterman 1985: 109), and to be the potential and rightful sexual consumer of the women among them (Biardeau 1972: 73). Other similar images are evoked in Sanskritic descriptions of royal installations where the element of exporting the violence of revivification comes to the fore. Thus we are told that, after the sacrificial phase of the ritual, the king should set out on symbolic expeditions of conquest towards his neighbours, expeditions which are partly wars and partly hunts (Heesterman 1985: 119–20). In other words, because of the royal symbolism of sacrifice recalled by the association with Vishnu, all the symbolic evocations we have seen acted out in the triumphalist ends of other rituals of rebounding violence from other parts of the world are also present in Hindu ritual.

However, just as the rebounding violence cannot ever be isolated from the initial violence, the sacrificial image cannot be separated from the ascetic image in Hindu ritual. This also means that, at least in historical times, it has never been possible to envisage the image of the king as triumphant sacrificer as legitimate on its own. As is well known, in Hindu political theory the king must always be associated with the Brahman or the ascetic because it is only thanks to the co-operation between Brahman and king that sacrifice can be performed.[1] Thus, it is the duty of the Brahman to prepare the sacrifice, as it is the duty of the king to reap its fruits. The Brahman is given the ascetic task of the attack on native vitality, the first part of rebounding violence, and the king aggressively recovers vitality from external beings whom he consumes, the second part of rebounding violence.

By re-enacting sacrifice in funerary and other rituals the Hindu participants are therefore transforming themselves from the ascetic of the first part into the king of the second part, from Siva to Vishnu and from prey into hunter.[2]

Sociologically, the significance of this movement shows how the complete continuity between practices which we normally think of as typically religious, such as sacrifice, and the political is achieved. The intermediate step elides the two by making an instrumental religious act appear as part of a general cosmic enterprise, and this inevitably involves a theory of the polity.

In Hinduism the notion of cosmogony implies a theory of the state, but this specific formulation hides a much more general principle found in all the cases so far examined. For example we saw how Buid sacrifice and spirit mediumship implies a theory that the community should defend itself from external predation by sharing and undifferentiation. What the Buid do to cure disease, therefore, at the same time specifies the forms of institutionalisation they consider legitimate.

However, noting the homology between political idioms and religious idioms is still a long way from understanding the practical political effects of these idioms; to do this it is necessary to turn again to actual cases. The profane implications of this connection between the religious and the political are not easily seen in contemporary India where the political effectiveness of Hindu polities has, for the most part, long ago disappeared. In order to show, therefore, that this final link in the chain of connections which this book seeks to establish also exists in systems which present themselves as concerned with the whole cosmos, I turn to a not altogether unrelated example, that of Japan.

One of the best-known aspects of contemporary Japanese culture is that it has two religions which function in tandem, Shintoism and Buddhism. This state of affairs was very largely intentionally created following the dramatic events of the Meiji restoration; that is, the restoration of imperial rule in the nineteenth century.[3] The co-occurrence of two religions is somewhat surprising for people used to the Semitic religions with their jealous god, and so western writers have tended to consider this as an oddity. In fact something akin to this doubling occurs in somewhat similar forms throughout the Buddhist world and has led to much controversy as anthropologists have discussed how far the two 'religions' are really distinct (e.g. Tambiah 1970).

This duality takes many forms. For example, traditional Japanese houses contain at least two contrasting shrines: one a miniature Shinto shrine made of unvarnished wood and the other a lacquered, ancestral Buddhist shrine, which contains tablets with the names of previous generations of the caretakers of the house. These domestic shrines are miniatures of the public places of worship. Thus, in most of rural Japan, the most obvious manifestation of the two religions is the coexistence in the same locality of both Buddhist temples and Shinto shrines, which are patronised by the same people. In some cases the two kinds of places of worship occur side by side.

The geographical and architectural appearance of these temples and shrines is revealing in many ways. Traditional Japanese villages have clearly marked boundaries which often separate the inhabited area from the surrounding forest. The Buddhist temples and the Shinto shrines on the other hand usually cross this boundary, thus linking the outside with the inside. This is made possible by the fact that both are constructed as alleyways with buildings, gates and lamps marking a long central avenue of usually at least several hundred yards. It is this image of the alleyway crossing a boundary which can best enable us to understand the religious significance of the two types of places of worship.

Buddhist temples are organised along a central path across which various buildings are found. The path is clearly marked on the ground and is further emphasised by lanterns and paired sculptures such as the guard dogs[4] which serve to mark the beginning of the alleyway. This central alleyway leads via a gate to an inner sanctum in which a Buddhist image is placed. In some cases, however, the actual temple itself appears as merely the continuation of the path and this effect is achieved quite deliberately by placing a long canopy which links the path to the main building and which is said to represent the continuity of ordinary humans and Buddhas. The use of the appearance of the building to express a religious message shows how the general linear appearance of the temple is far from accidental. The temple should be a permanent open way by which the inhabitants can renounce the world by leaving it. The alleyway architecture of the temple therefore expresses the central idea that Buddhism is the teaching of a 'path' facilitating renunciation of vitality, whether this be through meditation or through worship.

However, most forms of Japanese Buddhism have also other, less clearly orthodox themes than simple renunciation. These concerns are centrally involved with guiding the dead to paradise in a final journey. Among most Japanese the idea of the journey to paradise is not, as among other Buddhists, contradicted by simultaneously held beliefs in reincarnation (Dale Saunders 1964). This exit theme is particularly prominent in the two schools of Japanese Buddhism – Jodo Shu and Jodo Shin Shu – which have the greatest numbers of adherents. The 'Jodo' of their names means 'pure land' or 'paradise' and this reflects the fact that helping the dead reach paradise is their central concern.[5] For these schools at least, the journey of Buddhism marked by the central path of the temples combines the path of renunciation with the path which the ancestors will follow, with the stress being more on this second aspect.

The journey which Buddhism facilitates actually begins before death and continues after it. It is really only in old age, however, that concern with this final journey begins to be of importance for ordinary people. The importance of Buddhism for the old manifests itself in the ideal that the final period of life should literally be occupied by an extended but nonetheless real journey. This happens when the old begin to go on a series of pilgrimages to famous monasteries. Although each pilgrimage is separate, the various pilgrimages can also be thought of as all part of a general journey of renunciation through Buddhism. This process is envisaged as part of a willing self-renunciation since the pilgrimages are a preparation for death. In this Buddhism is similar to Hinduism since pilgrimage to Benares as well as the taking of a corpse to Benares is seen as a conscious action of the dying by which they make their death a willed and organised act of renunciation.

In Japan, however, the journey of old age out of this life tends to involve a number of journeys to monasteries, which are seen as part of one long series culminating in death. The stages in this continuous series of pilgrimages are recorded by prayers calligraphed by monks at the various monasteries onto a large scroll or a notebook carried by the pilgrim and subsequently occasionally displayed at Buddhist rituals. These records gradually fill up, but should only become complete at death. In this way, because the series of pilgrimages has been begun before death, the journey which will follow after death can be seen as merely the continuation of a process which had begun as a result of the free choice of the worshipper. After death the continuation of the journey becomes more complicated in that the body and the soul separate. However, the pilgrimage idiom still dominates for both.

The disposal of the body is taken care of by Buddhist monks. Theirs is the task of taking it out of the house to a cemetery for burial or for cremation. In either case the decomposition and disappearance of the corpse is marked by Buddhist rites especially focused on various boundaries such as the threshold of the house, the entrance to the cemetery or place of cremation, and so on. The laity regard it as the task of the monks in these circumstances to remove the pollution and the weakness of death from the house of the dead and from the living. This is done partly through ritual purification and partly by the monks taking the pollution upon themselves. The body is then sometimes first commemorated by a memorial of perishable wood, but the place of the remains is finally marked by a small stone monument which bears a devotional Buddhist message and a posthumous Buddhist name. Often these stone memorials are in an area adjoining the temples.

The disposal and ultimate elimination of the soul of the dead is also a Buddhist concern. It has two sides. One side concerns the soul's invisible journey, while the other concerns the making and then disposal of the ancestral tablet. Immediately after death the invisible soul of the dead person is believed to be unwilling to leave the house and the community of the living and so it must be cajoled, forced or even tricked into going. This process again requires the services of Buddhism, which will help the soul to surrender the vital. Because of the central role of Buddhist monks in all this, it is not surprising that for ordinary people Buddhism is, by and large, a system for the removal of the dead, whether in body or spirit, and because of this, it and its clergy always retain a somewhat inauspicious image (Embree 1939: 261).

The association of Buddhism with death and the dead is common to many parts of the Buddhist world and Tambiah describes a somewhat similar situation in Thailand (Tambiah 1970). However, this goes even further in Japan, to the extent that the ancestors are always referred to by the word used for Buddha, *Hotoke*, and ordinary people primarily think of ancestors when this word is used (Smith 1974: 53–4). Similarly the objects of Buddhist worship are almost exclusively beings concerned with the guiding of the dead soul to the western paradise. The most important Buddha for the Jodo schools and, indeed, for most Japanese Buddhists is Amida, the guardian of the 'pure land'. The stress on Amida is such that some writers have said that this type of Japanese Buddhism is not really 'Buddhism' at all but 'Amidism' (Embree 1939: 230). Amida is principally seen as a guide who facilitates the entry of the soul into the pure land. Together with the incarnated Buddha, Kannon, who is carely distinguishable from Amida in the popular mind, he is the central figure in the domestic Buddhist shrines, where he represents the possibility of exit for the dead.

However, the image of the companion along a path is perhaps clearest of all in the case of the almost equally important Bodisattva Jizo. Jizo is explicitly believed to guide souls towards paradise, especially those souls who might have difficulty in leaving this life and who might therefore cause trouble to those they refuse to leave behind. This explains Jizo's close association with aborted embryos and young children who, because they have not yet enjoyed vitality, are thought to be unwilling to go along the path of renunciation and therefore require Jizo's kindly guidance (Smith 1974: 49). Jizo is so much associated with passage that his shrines are found at crossroads and entrances of all kinds, especially at the entrances of cemeteries. The cult of Jizo and to a lesser extent of Amida, and indeed of most Japanese Buddhism, is, therefore, a cult intended to facilitate the complex journey of the invisible soul after death, partly for its own benefit and partly to stop it from bothering the living. This is so in spite of the fact that, unlike other Mahayana Buddhists, ordinary Japanese seem little interested in the nature of the journey.

The journey of the soul, however, also takes on a visible form and this is where the alleyway architecture of the temple comes into its own. In fact it is not just the large temple which is involved but also the miniature temple,[6] which should be found in most traditional houses. These miniature temples are to a certain extent also constructed along a central path. Leading to the miniature temple are a number of steps and inside the staircase continues, leading to a central figure, usually of Kannon or of Amida.

Shortly after death a lacquered tablet should be made to commemorate and represent the soul of the dead. The movements of that tablet both reflect and facilitate the journey of the soul. After death the tablet will be placed in front of the miniature lacquered Buddhist temple, then, after a time, it will ascend the first step leading inwards and upwards, then, rising every few months step by step the tablet will finally reach the inside of the miniature temple. There it will remain for many years and there it will receive a kind of worship. The journey of the ancestral tablet is therefore like that of the invisible soul and of the body, an outward journey, but it is a very slow journey where the element of expulsion is played down for some time.

This worship, which the tablet receives, could not be more different from, for example, African ancestor worship, where the blessing and presence of the ancestors is actively sought, or even from the much more ambiguous ancestor worship of people like the Orokaiva. The point of Japanese ancestor worship is, rather, to placate the ancestors by sharing with them to a certain extent, for example by offering a little food on a daily basis. This sharing, however, occurs only because it is not yet possible to get rid of the dead completely. Japanese ancestor worship is above all concerned with the removal of the pollution which the dead inevitably imply, and, above all, with sending the ancestors on their way, however unwilling they might be to go (Smith 1974: 40ff.).

The ambiguity of this worship is particularly evident during the annual *Bon* festival. This festival, which lasts a few days in summer, is an occasion when the ancestors' souls are called to rejoin their tablets and to re-enter their house. During this period much more important food offerings are made at the ancestral miniature temple and Buddhist monks are called into the house to say more significant prayers. This is something which is normally avoided at all cost because of the monks' association with death. The period of welcome to the ancestors is, however, tense and short-lived. After a few days the offerings that were made to the tablets during the festival are surreptitiously taken to the boundary of the inhabited area in the hope that the ancestors will follow the food and not notice what is happening.[7] Finally these offerings are dumped near a stream which flows away from the territory so that the spirit of the dead will foolishly follow and be swept away.[8] Then and only then do the real festivities begin. *Bon* is therefore not so much a celebration of the ancestors as a celebration of their expulsion.

Indeed, in the end, in areas such as the lake Biwa area, the house will be rid of the ancestors altogether. After a number of years, and with the help of the monks, the tablet will be taken out of the miniature temple in the house and placed on the larger outward-bound alleyway that is the community temple proper, there to remain.

In this way all the forms of outward journeys brought about by Buddhism join together and all can, to a certain extent, be considered as forms of attacks on, and renunciations of, vitality. The role of Japanese Buddhism in practical religion is equivalent to the first part of rituals such as Orokaiva initiation or Dinka sacrifice; it is the equivalent of Buid spirit mediumship or Hindu cremation. It is essentially a matter of organising the loss of vitality and making the actor co-operate with its loss. Unlike our earlier examples, it is not a part of a ritual system, but a total system designed to help the Japanese Buddhist attack his or her living self and begin to take it away on its journey towards death, a journey which will continue when the body is taken by the monks. The outward journey will be completed when, in the form of an ancestor represented by the inscribed tablet, the dead will be taken out through the miniature temple to the main exit of the main temple.

Japanese Buddhism therefore brings about the first violence of rebounding conquest and this is manifested in many ways. For the living it is self-inflicted violence and it takes the form of the requirement for ascetic and punishing pilgrimage and, in the case of monks at least, meditation, which often requires preliminary attacks on the body such as beatings, fasting or submitting to frights. For the dead the violence is administered by those who remain and it takes the form of the trickery which is required to get the soul away after death and after *Bon* and in other forms of expulsion.

However, if popular Japanese Buddhism is entirely concerned with the first part of rebounding violence, this does not mean that the second part does not also occur. Rather it is taken care of by those practices which since the Meiji restoration have been separated from Buddhism and grouped together under the label of Shintoism.

In contrast to Buddhism, Shintoism is not a religion as we tend to understand the word, but rather a class of somewhat similar cults.[9] However, Shintoism does share one thing with Buddhism, that is, the emphasis on the idea of a path, and this path is also materialised in the architecture of the places of worship. The very word *Shinto* means 'the path of the god' and, of the characters used for writing the name, one stands for god and the other for path or alleyway.

The architectural representation of the path of Shinto takes many forms. Most important is the significance of the famous *torii* or gateway which is the essential part of any Shinto shrine. This is so to the extent that the *torii* is recognised as the symbol of Shinto and that on Japanese maps the conventional sign for a shrine is a *torii*, rather as a cross marks a church on western maps.

The *torii* marks the beginning of the central way along which every part of the shrine is organised; it is what makes the shrine an alleyway. In fact, most Shinto shrines do not just have one such gateway but a number of them, sometimes ten or even more, and they all mark and emphasise the central path. This path is further dramatised by a number of pairs of objects placed on either side of the central alley, especially lanterns, and by the careful way in which its edge is lined with stones. The *torii* lead, via a variable number of intermediate buildings, to the sanctum itself. This most sacred of buildings proves on inspection to be merely a continuation of the alleyway, an almost perpetual recession where every part leads to yet a further enclosure. The sanctum is, therefore, a kind of tunnel which ultimately leads to a symbol of the god of the shrine. This symbol is not seen by worshippers, but is hidden either behind closed doors or behind a bamboo curtain. The fact that, since the Meiji restoration at least, what lies in the shrine is but a symbol, which is an indicator of something outside, yet further away, again emphasises the shrine as a narrow tunnel to the beyond. The god to which the symbol in the shrine refers may be the site at Ise where the imperial family is believed to have come to earth, or simply, the forest beyond the boundary of the locality, since the god is often a natural feature: a forest, a mountain, a waterfall or even a tree.

I have written so far as if the shrines led out of the locality and into the wilderness since this is how they appear at first; in fact, however, they are leading in exactly the opposite direction. The alleyway that is the shrine does lead out, but it is above all intended to be a path which serves for the *entry* of the power of the god to the inhabited area. The presence of the shrine in the locality is thus an open invitation to the god to come in and benefit the people. Thus the worshippers at a shrine stand either closer or further away in the alleyway, and from there they call the god to come so that they may receive its incoming strength and vitality. Similarly the role of the Shinto priest in all the rituals is to call in this flow of vitality through invocation, sacred dance or, sometimes, a medium.

Shintoism is about the bringing in of the strengthening force of a god to a specific social group so that the group may succeed unimpaired and continue through time. Shintoism is a cult of the strengthening of life, growth, and fertility in all its forms and it concerns those who can be considered the proper containers of that vital strength: the young and those at the height of their physical powers. Shinto gods are therefore invoked for all occasions which require growth and strength, such as new year ceremonies, agricultural fertility rites, the annual boys' and girls' festivals, weddings, starting businesses, going to school or university and, above all, celebrations of the founders of social communities (Ono 1962: 62).

The apparently individual strengthening of some of these concerns is misleading since Ono, a practitioner and apologist for Shinto, makes quite clear that the concern of Shintoism is the continuity of communities, whether these be descent groups or local groups or the nation. Shinto may be concerned with the strengthening of individuals but this is because these individuals are the suitable agents of the strength of the social group, whether this be a local community, a descent group or the whole nation. The gods of Shinto therefore maintain and increase the life force which exists in a social agent, which is a corporate group and whose existence transcends the presence of the individual representatives of that agent at any particular time.

Equally revealing of its nature is what Shinto is opposed to. Any contact with individual death, illness or any other form of weakness or misfortune is highly damaging and polluting to Shinto.[10] Shinto is not about strengthening the weak; it is about strengthening the strong. This means that an essential preliminary of Shinto cults involves elaborate purification and strengthening through ordeal to remove the worshipper from the contacts which he or she might have had with weakness or death pollution: *kegare*. Thus, people with wounds or illness cannot go to shrines. These restrictions are even more emphatic for Shinto priests and they are forbidden, for example, to attend the funerals of even their closest kin, while, for their part, monks may not even enter the shrines.[11]

The antipathy of Shintoism to anything that might be polluting or weakening is also revealed by the way the gates of the small domestic Shinto shrines must remain tightly shut when anybody is ill or dying. This is especially the case for the *Bon* festival when, as we saw, the spirits of the dead are momentarily recalled to the house.

Indeed, what happens at *Bon* is particularly revealing about the relationship of Buddhism and Shintoism. As noted above, the first part of *Bon* concerns the ancestors and is therefore a matter to be dealt with by Buddhism. This is so right up to the final stage of the ritual when the ancestors are unceremoniously expelled. However, in most cases their expulsion is followed by very different rituals. These are triumphalist, strengthening Shinto rituals.[12] In one case which I was able to observe in the lake Biwa area, such a ritual was focused on representative young men from the main houses in the community. First they were purified, then, at the Shinto shrine they participated in the usual communion with the priests where the participants drink rice wine out of unglazed earthenware.[13] Then the youths set out from the shrine armed with burning flares with which they engaged in mock battles with other youths. Finally, having reached a little sacred woodland on the boundary of the

community, the youths competitively threw their lighted flares into the trees to
see who could place theirs highest. The point of this last part of the ritual was
that in the past, and perhaps still today, this competitive display of strength
led to a good harvest.

Such a ritual is a good illustration of the chracter of Shintoism as it contains
most of its central elements. Above all, it expresses the idea that the young men
are the representatives of the strength and the future reproduction of the
community and that Shinto is there to maintain this strength and increase it.
The ritual also illustrates the direction of the flow of the power of the god of
the shrine. In the shrine the god is invoked by the priest so that it will come *into*
the locality via the alleyway in order to strengthen the young men. Then,
having been strengthened, the young men continue the outward direction
towards the boundary of the community in a way that demonstrates their
vigour, the fertility of their enterprises and their aggressiveness.

Shintoism, therefore, acts out the rebound of the very different first violence
of Buddhism. This first violence was directed against the vitality of the older
members of the community. The rebounding violence of Shintoism on the
other hand concerns the young and the strong and it is outwardly directed,
fertile and aggressive. The ritual of *Bon*, by making the violence of Shintoism
follow the violence of Buddhism, shows well how the two are linked, in the
same way as the renunciation of Hindu death is followed by cosmogonic
sacrifice. It is not difficult to understand why both Buddhism and Shintoism
use a path as their main symbol and also why movement along these paths
occurs in opposite directions. The path of Buddhism is the path of the exit of
vitality and the path of Shintoism is the path of its triumphal and forward-
looking return.

We are here back with the same two-way movement first identified in the
case of Orokaiva initiation. In the Orokaiva case this began with the exit from
the locality of the initiates, an exit which is represented as the willing surrender
of vitality, and which concludes with their vital triumphal return. In both
cases this concluding, socially strengthening return itself turns outwards as it
threatens other communities with its valour. As in the Japanese case the
significance of this final part is left ambiguously hovering between the idiom of
successful reproduction and outwardly directed expansion.

At this point the reader might well think that in my eagerness to stress the
parallel between the various examples I am ignoring a number of fundamental
differences between a case such as Orokaiva initiation and Japan.

Firstly, it might be argued that, while among the Orokaiva it is the young
who are principally concerned with the outward journey and that it is the
adults who recover vitality in the return journey, in Japan it is the old and the
dead who leave and the young who benefit from rebounding conquest. This,
however, would be to forget the corporate ideology of both societies. Among
the Orokaiva the initiates are as much representatives of the whole community
as they are one person when they are 'killed' by the ancestors. This means that

submitting to the conquest of the ancestors is something which will be repeated throughout life and will be clearest at death when this conquest will be final. Similarly, among the Japanese, it should be remembered that, in Shintoism, the young conquerors stand, as Ono stressed, for the vitality and continuity of the whole community.

Secondly it might be argued that, while among the Orokaiva it is the spirits of the dead who return as conquerors, in the village in Japan it is the strength emanating from the gods which enters via the alleyway of Shintoism. These gods might be thought to be quite different from the dead ancestors whom the Japanese try to coax into leaving. It could therefore be argued that in Japan there is no real connection between the outward and inward movement of vitality.

In fact this difference is not as marked as it might appear, since, as many Japanese writers have pointed out, the Shinto spirits are often seen as the very ancestors who had been expelled through Buddhism. According to this way of thinking, after the purification which the Buddhist journey has brought about, the ancestors return as gods along the alleyway of the shrines (Yanagita 1946; Hori 1974: 52 ff.).

However, in Japan, unlike the case of the Orokaiva, it is not every ancestor who becomes a Shinto god. Those people whose souls can become gods are of two kinds. They are either people who were believed in life to have been brimming with vitality, whether good or evil, or they are those who can be seen to be at the source of the vitality of a social group. If their super-vitality was sufficiently strong then these exceptional persons do not need the long purification process of Buddhism and they can become gods immediately. Typical among these kinds of gods in the relatively modern period are the Emperor himself, who can be represented as the vital source of the Japanese nation, and the war dead, who can be thought of as having negated their death by making it 'life-giving'. These people become strength-giving gods directly and therefore never have anything to do with Buddhism (Smith 1974: 56–63).[14]

Thirdly, it could be argued that the violent element that we saw in the Orokaiva spirit return is perhaps not as obvious in Japanese religion. Normally, the Shinto gods do not return as hunters or as military leaders. However, once again this difference is not as fundamental as it might seem at first and this is so for two different reasons. The first reason is that the idea that the community, after having been strengthened by its gods, is a conqueror and consumer of external vitality is also present in the forms of Shintoism discussed above, although this idiom is somewhat different in kind and weaker than is the case in the Orokaiva ritual. For example, we saw how the end of one Shinto ritual involved a mock attack directed towards the outside by young people. This example could be duplicated in many instances but with local variations.

Secondly, the consumption element of rebounding violence is also present in Shintoism and, as for the Orokaiva, it takes the form of aggressive meat eating, or rather fish eating. Ordinary Japanese are very little given to abstract theological speculation, but one of the differences between Shinto shrines and Buddhist temples that is well known and often mentioned is that, while offerings to ancestors at Buddhist temples are strictly vegetarian, meals and offerings at shrines must include animal products, especially fish. The abstention from flesh in Buddhism is linked with the other-worldly character of the religion. The piscivorous aspect of Shintoism links up with the strength-giving aspect of carnivorous activities and is a general, implicit, but powerful theme of Japanese life.

One of the essential aspects of Shinto shrine worship is the celebratory meals where the same kinds of food as those offered to the gods are consumed. These meals clearly glorify the values of community and successful reproduction, but they also seem to stress how this reproduction is achieved through the complete consumption of the environment since they normally require thirteen different foods, including such items as rice wine, freshwater fish, seawater fish, wild land birds, water fowl, salt and so on.

Furthermore, in modern Japan the eating of raw fish and meat also takes on the form of a kind of secular aggressive ritual in certain types of restaurants or bars mainly patronised by men. There the theme of violent consumption is expanded to the extent that the fish needs to be shown to be alive immediately before it is eaten. Sometimes slices of it are eaten while it is still wriggling on the dish and sometimes the whole fish is eaten alive. It is difficult not to see in this type of activity a celebration of the conquest of other forms of life, which brings us back to the Orokaiva concluding feasts.

It is even possible to go further in the comparison with the Orokaiva case since in Japan we again find an association between the consumption of another species and the consumption of human flesh. For example, Smith tells us that the villagers of Kurusu would not eat broiled fish after funerals 'for even the insensitive will recognise an untoward reminder of the act of cremation' (Smith 1978: 157).

On closer examination the Japanese case does, therefore, appear to be fairly close to the Orokaiva example with which this book began. The element of violence involved in the renunciation of vitality leads to the return of vitality in a form which brings about aggressive reproduction of the community through consumption of the vitality of outsiders, whether other species or other humans. There is, however, a difference in the emphasis on the constituent elements of rebounding violence in the two cases. Clearly, when we look at Japanese domestic religion, the element of final conquest and violence is much more underplayed than in Orokaiva initiation. This is similar to the difference in degree of emphasis noted between Dinka sacrifice, where the expansionist theme was strong, and ordinary Hindu cremation, where it was weak.

In Hindu sacrifice as practised in contemporary Benares the element of aggressive regeneration was comparatively muted. It was only when we saw the connection of the cremations in Benares with the asceticism of Siva and the cosmogony of Vishnu, and the connection of these divine acts with the Hindu notions of kingship that the elements of conquest and consumption came as strongly to the fore as they do in Dinka sacrifice. This is not surprising. Throughout this book I have stressed that the rebounding of violence can either take a reproductive form in which vitality is regained from creatures such as pigs or cattle or an aggressive form in which this recovery becomes extended to involve more ambitious expansionist aims. In most cases the boundary between these two formulations is unclear, so that one can slip from one to the other imperceptibly. It is therefore easy to understand how, in the traditional Hindu idea of the kingdom, the same ritual of sacrifice was more a matter of reproduction when it was carried out by subjects and more a matter of aggression when carried out by kings.

This difference corresponds to the fact that, while the Orokaiva and the Dinka are stateless societies, Hindu kingdoms and Japan are state societies. Among the Orokaiva or the Dinka the political is in the hands of actors at the local level. This means that for these people it is local rituals which carry the full burden of creating the political entity. In state societies, just as we find a class division between a ruling class and subjects, we find a differentiation in the rituals proper to the two groups. This is not usually a fundamental differentiation and indeed the evocative power of the rituals of the rulers for the ruled largely depends on the connection these have with the symbolism by which ordinary citizens express their reproduction through rebounding conquest. What happens is that similar symbolic sequences are used by the two groups with different emphases which express different political idioms. Because the ruled are left with only a concern with their own reproduction, their rituals play down the expansionist potential of rebounding conquest. The rulers on the other hand can exploit this potential to the full, not only because, in certain circumstances, they can indulge in expansion against neighbours, but also because, given their situation, they are in a sense permanent consumers of those they control. Thus we find, as in India, very similar rituals at the local and the state level, but while at the local level the aggressive and expansionist element is played down, the opposite is true at the state or royal level.

We find the same situation in Japan. As noted above, the two-way movement of Buddhism and Shintoism in the traditional village can principally be thought of as a matter of the reproduction of local groups, but, for that very reason, it can also be applied to the whole nation represented as a super descent-cum-local group incarnated in the Emperor. What this meant in practice was that the ruling class was utilising the symbolism of rebounding violence, but in the name of the whole nation. When this symbolism is used in this way it is to be expected that we find its aggressive version always ready to come to the surface.

This is, of course, what happened after the Meiji restoration. Furthermore, because the history of Japan is well known, we can follow what happened during that period in order to understand the historical potential of the idiom of rebounding violence when it is in the hands of a particular class.

The period of Japanese isolation which had been maintained by the Shogunate into the second half of the nineteenth century came to an abrupt end, partly as a result of the incursion of the American so-called 'Black Ships', which broke the embargo. The feeling of national humiliation which this aroused led to the dramatic political changes of the Meiji restoration, after which the Emperor was placed in a unique and dominant position. These changes also had a religious aspect which is often represented as the replacement of a period dominated by the Buddhism of the Shogunate to one dominated by the Shintoism of the Emperor.

In fact things were much more complicated. The fortunes of the various sects of Buddhism and of the Shinto shrines had fluctuated wildly at different periods and the influence of Confucianism had been as important during some periods of the Shogunate as that of Buddhism. Furthermore, the development of Shintoism as a potentially nationalist cult of the Emperor and of nature had its origins at least as far back as the eighteenth century (Smith 1983, chapter 1). Nonetheless, some aspects of the traditional picture are accurate. For example, it was true that, as the reformers complained, there existed before the restoration a number of schools which were a complete mixture of what was to become Shintoism and Buddhism. Perhaps as far as practical religion was concerned the pre-Meiji restoration situation may not have been very different from that described above for the present day, but it is true that theological and institutional distinctions were not as clear as they later became.

Initially the restorers intended to bring about a sharp break with the past and they attempted to abolish Buddhism altogether and to replace it by what was presented as the ancient religion of Japan, but which was in fact a new one, called Shintoism. Shintoism was created out of a multitude of shrine cults which became subsidised and organised by the state and given a theological emphasis which owed a lot to the ideas of the European Enlightenment. Above all the new religion was focused on the Emperor and his family, thereby making Shintoism a kind of lineage cult which took in the whole nation (Smith 1983, chapter 1). Rapidly, however, the fundamental intention of the reformers totally to eradicate Buddhism foundered, but the emphasis remained on laws requiring the separation of Buddhism and Shintoism, which, it was argued, had become dangerously mixed up.

The failure of the attempt to abolish Buddhism in spite of strong government pressure is illuminating. It repeated the failure of many previous attempts to get rid of either the shrine cults or Buddhism. The impression we get is that whatever the politicians or the ideologues might have wanted, ordinary people could not do without both systems. This would follow indeed from the analysis given above, which emphasises the totally complementary nature of the two systems. Put less abstractly, the problem that the abolition of Buddhism presented was that, in spite of attempts to bypass the difficulty (Smith 1974: 73–4), Shinto had no way of dealing with weakening and death. The only possibility, therefore, was to accept the presence of the two religions, but to insist on the separation of Shintoism and Buddhism and make Shintoism the religion of the state and the Emperor. Renunciation on the part of the subjects and of the Buddhist monks could then lead to the rebounding vitality of the Emperor in much the way the renunciation of the Hindu Brahman could lead to the conquering sacrificial strength of the king.

The purpose of this separation, which brought about the state of affairs I discussed above, was to revitalise the nation by freeing the strength-giving side from the weakening, death-polluted, spiritual side. This separation was, therefore, a kind of cranking up of the machinery of rebounding violence by 'straightening the pathways', a matter of clearing the exit to the other world and consequently, and more significantly, of clearing the way for the entrance of the returning spirits for their reconsumption of strength and flesh.

The separation of Buddhism and Shintoism and the acceleration of the two-way system also had its alimentary aspect. Significantly the Meiji restoration led to the abolition of Buddhist vegetarian laws. Furthermore, the development of the fish-eating voracity discussed above seems to have been an indirect result of the intensification of the contrast between Buddhism and Shintoism.

The success of the Meiji restoration as a re-establishment of national purpose is of course well known and not explicable by ideological factors alone, but there is no doubt that the religious reforms were intended to achieve this national strengthening. Furthermore, the 'cranking up' which these religious reforms ultimately legitimised encouraged the movement towards the militarist and imperialist idiom, which reached its apogee during the greater East Asia war. This is very significant in that it shows how rebounding violence, which in certain contexts may be simply a matter of assuring the image of the continuation of permanent institutional structures by a special image of reproduction, can, *under certain circumstances* develop into a profound and convincing legitimation of actual political and military expansionism.

First of all there is what may be called the internal distribution of the versions of rebounding violence within state structures. There, as we saw, the more humble reproductive versions are to be found among the dominated, while the potentially more aggressive versions are elaborated by the ruling class. When the external conditions which normally encouraged the aggressive variant are found, the acting out of the second variant by the ruling class appears appropriate to all and involves in its dynamism the dominated classes, who recognise in it both their own reproductive ideology and its expansionist potential. This double recognition is what welds the rulers to the ruled and leads to the legitimation of aggressiveness by the ruling class, which is both directed towards the outside and towards the ruled, but which can appear, for a while at least, as a joint national purpose.

All this of course is not say that the existence of the symbolism of rebounding violence is in any way a sufficient explanation of the outbreak of real political or military violence. Japanese militarist expansionism was very largely caused by contact with western imperialism. However, given these circumstances, the religious process naturally gave an idiom to such expansionism and may well have exacerbated it. After all, consuming external vitality for one's higher spiritual purposes is the way militarism and expansionism have always represented themselves.

The continuity between individual and group practices concerned with death, the fertility of crops and so on, and ideologies of the state in both the Hindu and the Japanese cases shows how rebounding violence can imperceptibly glide from individual instrumental rituals to general cosmic systems which imply general political principles. This is what explains why a curing ritual can become the occasion for an aggressive raid among the Dinka, and how the religious aspect of Japanese Emperors explains the aggressive idiom of some recent Japanese history.

The historical perspective which the Japanese example furnishes does, however, enable us to understand better the actual political implications of rebounding violence. It shows that the idiom of the system furnishes a potential which can be exploited under circumstances which are quite external to the ideas of rebounding violence. It was not the mixing up of Buddhism and Shintoism which led to the end of the Shogunate but developments in the world economic system which led to the American incursion. However, that incursion led to an intensification of the contrast and the connection between the first part of rebounding conquest, the renunciation of native vitality, and the second part, the consumption of external vitality. It was as though the implications of the whole system that were already present had been tensioned by events. This manifested itself in the separation of Buddhism and Shintoism and the development of the imperial cult. This in turn, when politico-economic conditions made it possible, led to the transformation of the reproductive form of rebounding conquest into the aggressive form, a potential we have already seen in the Dinka case. However, because in the Japanese case a large and important state was involved, the results of this change had world significance.

5

Marriage

In the previous three chapters the theme of 'rebounding violence' has been examined in very different parts of the world and has been seen to be present in such varied ritual phenomena as sacrifice, initiation, spirit possession and funerary rituals.

The dramatic representation of rebounding violence in rituals often utilises animals closely associated with humans in order to achieve its effect. Most often these are domesticated animals. This is because such animals can serve to represent identification at one moment and alienation at the next. In the rituals these animals initially evoke non-transcendental vitality in humans and the driving out of this element from the subject's body is dramatised by chasing and finally killing the animal. Once the animal has been killed, its significance in the ritual can be transformed so that the very same animal now merely represents an external vitality, which is consumed by the participants as food, though this is regarded as extremely special and strength-giving food. It is this potential for symbolic transformation which is the key to the role of such animals in ritual.

Thus we saw how for the Dinka killing an animal, an action equated with the 'killing' of the innate cattle aspect of the human sacrificer, brought him or her close to Divinity because, without the cattle element, the sacrificer was left with only the other element of which human beings consist: pure, disembodied, truth-carrying speech, which is a manifestation of Divinity. Because a human being is not alive without the vital cattle element, the residual divine had to be recombined with vitality to make the sacrificer an active person again. In order to do this he or she followed the symbolic expulsion of the cattle aspect from his or her body by the actual recovery of this aspect by eating the meat of the killed animal, an action which was at the same time a promise and a celebration of future killing and possible victory over enemies and neighbours.

However, in the Dinka case and others like it, the killing of the animal and the eating of the meat evoke other associations over and beyond the consumption of vitality, enemies and outsiders. Those other associations can serve as an introduction to the subject matter of this chapter.

In these ethnographic examples the combination of continuities and discontinuities represented in the rituals as existing between animals and humans is made to recall another similar paradox: the continuities and discontinuities between female and male humans. This explains why, in a number of cases, (and this would include the Dinka) ritual symbolism collapses the two oppositions into a merged multivocalic evocation. In such cases the drama which reflects and constructs the internal battle in all participants, whether male or female, is not only represented, as it would be among the Orokaiva, by reference to such creatures as pigs and birds, but also by allusion to a ritual representation of parallel differences and similarities between men and women. In many cases both dichotomies – animals and humans and women and men – are used in counterpart and this seems to be the case with the Dinka.

The association of cattle with femininity among the Dinka might at first sight be surprising since it was noted in the last chapter that cattle are above all linked with virility and young men. Thus we saw how young men imitate cattle in their dances and how the horns of cattle are often fairly explicit phallic symbols, especially in the image of the bull who gouges the ground. In fact Dinka cattle are associated with both femaleness and maleness and this ambiguity is central to their ritual use.

Perhaps the most obvious female association of cattle is linked to their role in marriage. As is the case for many other African peoples, Dinka cattle are disposed of in one of three ways. They may be inherited, they may be killed in sacrifice, or they may be given in bridewealth in exchange for brides. It is this latter use which associates them with women, and not only with any women, but especially with women who are outsiders to the descent group. This is because the rules of incest and exogamy forbid men to marry women of their own group.

As the members of a Dinka lineage look on their cattle (animals which, as we saw, they intimately associate with their vitality, virility and strength), they know that these animals will either be killed in a symbolic abandonment of virile vitality or that they will ultimately be relinquished to outsiders in exchange for the future wives of members of their group. They also know that, in the past and in the future, they will themselves similarly receive cattle in exchange for the abandoned women of their descent group, their sisters and daughters who have had to leave to marry outsiders. Dinka cattle thus signify both the abandonment of the natal internal female element of the lineage, in so far as they were obtained in exchange for daughters and sisters, and the promise of external women, who will be obtained as wives and who will thus become the means by which the lineage will legitimately reproduce its own vitality through its children.

Now, this exchange of an internal vitality abandoned for an external vitality which is then internalised and becomes life-giving is, of course, immediately reminiscent of the pattern of rebounding violence as it was analysed in the rituals discussed in the previous chapters. This similarity between the effects of exogamy and the ritual formulations of rebounding violence is not merely formal. In the Dinka case the two systems colour each other by symbolic associations which are more or less explicit. This is particularly clear when we turn to an aspect of Dinka sacrifice which has not yet been discussed.

The Dinka sacrifice both male and female cattle, but for the most significant sacrifices they kill only male cattle. This masculinity is, however, required not so much for itself but so that it can be *transformed* during the ritual into femininity, a transformation which is reminiscent of the way that the virile young animals of the herd, by being given in bridewealth, are transformed into wives. This sexual transformation of cattle is perhaps only a minor theme, but a number of details of what is actually done during the ritual are explained by it. The sacrificial animal is literally changed from male to female. This is done in the following way. First of all, it is dressed in a girl's skirt during the weakening process of invocation. Secondly, its horns, seen as its most virile feature, are said to 'wilt' during the invocation. Finally, after the animal is killed its genitals are cut off to render it female (Lienhardt 1961: 268–9).

These apparently surprising aspects of Dinka sacrifice become understandable in terms of the more general pattern of rebounding violence. Usually cattle represent the native vitality of the group and this is expressed by the association of cattle with young men. This vital masculinity finds its expression particularly in the admiration directed towards the horns of the animal and we also find that the care of cattle is an almost exclusively male activity, while women are forbidden contact with the herd. Before the ritual, cattle are therefore predominantly a male symbol. However, the point of the first part of the ritual is to weaken the vitality that the cattle represent. This weakening is at the same time a weakening of virility. Hence the Dinka tell us that during the invocation the cattle's horns droop. It is during this time, when the animal is being defeated by the invocation, that the sacrificial animal is beginning to be feminised.

We do not have far to look for the reasons. First of all, the Dinka associate femininity with military weakness. Secondly, and even more importantly, they associate the loss of native vitality with the loss of their girls at marriage. It is, therefore, highly appropriate that, as native vitality is weakened in the ritual, it should be feminised and that when this native vitality is totally lost, at the moment when the sacrificial animal is killed, it should be made totally female by the special form of butchering which is then carried out.

Here, however, another aspect of the significance of this feminisation is revealed. As the animal is killed in the ritual, its identification with the sacrificer ends, and it becomes the meat of another species which can be safely consumed by humans. Consequently, the created femininity of the sacrificial animal also becomes an external, consumable femininity. This offers an exact parallel to the fact that when the lineage-grown girls become fully mature as females they are lost as wives to outsiders. At the moment when the animal has become fully feminine it also becomes foreign. The meat that is eaten is, therefore, both feminine meat and foreign in that it is the meat of an animal.

The parallel goes further. Because wives are very largely obtained with the cattle one has gained by abandoning one's own girls, it is experientially appropriate that in the ritual the loss of the internal feminine should lead to the taking of the external feminine in the form of consumed meat since, in the ritual, the very moment of separation, the killing, becomes the beginning of the recovery by rebounding violence of external vitality.

This recovered vitality is represented in the ritual as being of the same kind as that which was lost: it is a cattle element which was lost and it is a cattle element which is regained. But although the recovered vitality is of the same kind it is not in the same state and has lost its symbolical affiliation with the sacrificial group. Similarly, as a result of the rule of lineage exogamy, the lineage-grown girls who are lost in marriage are similar to those who will be obtained, except for the fact that they can be sexually consumed because they have a different social identity.[1]

It is therefore not surprising to find in Dinka sacrifice a subtle interpretation of the symbolism of gender and exogamy and that of cattle and it is this which explains the fact that cattle are associated with *both* virility and femininity, in that cattle are transformed during different stages in the ritual.

There is another way of looking at this whole matter which does not concentrate on the objects of the ritual, i.e. the cattle, but rather on the experience of the subjects, i.e. the sacrificers. Because, in the first part of sacrifice, there is an association between sacrificer and victim, the sacrificer therefore also starts as male and is then weakened and hence feminised. Finally, when the animal is killed, the association of sacrificer and victim is broken and the sacrificer is again represented as a male consumer of a female victim. Perhaps the whole matter appears less strange if we bear in mind that in a society such as that of the Dinka the individual, in this case the sacrificer, is largely continuous with his lineage, which contains both women and men. This means that any Dinka's personality contains an element which is not permanently gender-specific and which can therefore appear at one moment predominantly male and at another predominantly female.

This example is far from unusual and the same invocation of the theme of gender in complex representations of rebounding violence can be found in the some of the other examples already discussed. In Japan the gender assocations of the dual religious system are many and well known. For example there is a tendency in Japanese Buddhism to represent the Boddhisatvas who facilitate the renunciation of the world, such as Kannon, Amida and Jizo, as female, even though in their original forms they were usually represented as males. By way of contrast Shintoism has a strongly male character. For example many Shinto deities were represented in the past by little statuettes of erect phalluses and, although this type of practice has been disapproved of since the Meiji restoration, it has not totally died out. Similarly, women who are not virgins, especially menstruating women, are excluded from many aspects of the cults. Significantly the only Shinto cult in which women who are potential child-bearers have any significant role is marriage. Indeed, in modern Japan it would not be totally wrong to say that Shintoism has become a cult of marriage and that marriage is often seen as part of a triumphal consumption of the female by the male.

It is not surprising, therefore, to find that in societies where marriage involves one spouse being absorbed into the family of the other and where the rule of incest is expanded to become a rule of group exogamy, a tie-up occurs between the symbolism of rebounding conquest and that of marriage and gender. In these cases the incoming spouse and her gender takes or joins the symbolic place held by animals in other systems. We need not, therefore, be too taken aback that so many people around the world, from African to South East Asia, talk of the taking of spouses from outside as 'eating' them. In other words, marriage and exogamy in these cases can be viewed as simply other manifestations of that wider underlying process of rebounding conquest which we saw already implied in initiation, sacrifice, spirit possession and so on.

This merging is not an external observer's view imposed on the data. If anything anthropologists have been over-zealous in separating phenomena which others see as forming a whole and have thereby caused unnecessary if famous controversies. For example, the famous *tali* tying ritual of the Nayars has been variously interpreted as an initiation (Gough 1955) and as a marriage (Gough 1959), as though it could not be both. Other similar conjunctions abound in the ethnographic literature. Thus, in a recent study of New Ireland, the ethnographer concluded that the symbolism of marriage and that of sacrifice were merely two sides of the same thing (Kuchler 1985). In making these associations between marriage and sacrifice or marriage and initiation I am, therefore, merely following the implications of the language by which marriage and exogamy are talked about in a wide range of cultures throughout the world.

In fact, the linked themes of death, transcendence, conquest, consumption and imperialist militarism, which were stressed in the previous chapters, are all to be found in very similar forms in many symbolical representations of gender and marriage.

To illustrate some of these points I shall turn to a recent ethnography from Ladakh, that part of North India which, in many ways, is a cultural extension of Tibet because it shares with Tibet a closely related language, many historical connections and above all the same religion, a form of Mahayana Buddhism. My choice is for two reasons. Firstly, the ethnography illustrates well many of the points which concern us here, although it is true that cases from many other different parts of the world would also do this. Secondly, the subtlety and penetrating analysis of the ethnographer, Maria Phylactou, makes my task much easier, especially as she is centrally concerned with some of the issues raised in this chapter (Phylactou 1989).

As in other parts of the Tibetan world the Ladakhi house and the household it contains is the prime social, political and symbolic unit of the society. The house is the source of identity for the people who live in it and they, to a certain extent and in certain contexts, can be considered as together forming a single social actor. As social units, houses are quite distinct from each other and their boundaries, separating as they do those who are in and those who are out, are rigidly maintained at both a practical and a symbolic level. Finally, the house is in many ways a temple in that all aspects of its structure have religious significance and the shrine to the household gods it contains is its actual and symbolic centre.

Houses are strictly exogamous and it is normally the girls who leave at marriage to enter the houses of their husbands. The marriage ritual therefore involves either the bringing in of a new bride or the relinquishing of a daughter. Given the great emphasis on the integrity of the house group and the ritual stressing of the physical boundaries of the building both operations are dramatic.

The first part of the ideal marriage ritual, the *bagston*, is focused on the expedition which sets out from the groom's house to fetch the bride from her house. This is done by a party of young men, sumptuously dressed, and preferably on horseback. They are led by one who is particularly well decked out and who carries an arrow. In some ways this party of wife-takers assumes aspects of a conquering, almost military, expedition while at the same time being messengers of the gods. These themes come to the surface in the dances of the young men (Phylactou 1989: 240) and the fact that their journey is sometimes said to re-enact a myth concerning the expedition of a culture hero, a mythical king, who recovers his bride from a foreign abductor and seducer. The hero kills the villain and takes back the woman. This myth is actually extremely complex, and Phylactou shows how in its detail it evokes many ambiguous aspects of marriage, but the references to the myth actually evoked during the ritual are relatively simple; above all they identify the party of the young fetchers of the bride with the king's companions.

On arrival the wife-takers seem to take on aspects of an invading party which the family of the wife attempts to hold back in a variety of ways. In some parts of Ladakh the bride's party builds a succession of small stone obstacles which have to be overcome (Phylactou 1989: 248). Sometimes the outsiders have to answer riddles before they are allowed to proceed. Sometimes they find the door barred. However, in the end, the groom's party, which is referred to as the 'outsiders', succeeds in penetrating the enclosed territory of the wife-givers, who are the 'insiders'.

When they finally enter the house the youths still have to face resistance from the girl's relatives, especially from the women, but these are finally defeated or successfully bribed by the invaders. Then the leader of the groom's party triumphantly plants the arrow he has been so prominently carrying in a bowl of grain, an action which is repeated a number of times in different contexts. Subsequently, he picks out the bride from a group of girls and sometimes literally hooks her with the arrow. From then on the party of wife-takers is concerned only with taking the bride away as quickly as possible in spite of the girl's much displayed sorrow at leaving her natal household and the shrine of her house where she will never again make offerings. As she takes leave of her relatives and her sometimes weeping brothers she says, 'I have become the daughter of a stranger.'

The groom's party takes the bride back to his house and there a triumphal celebration takes place, but it is one in which the bride can hardly participate. It will take time before she becomes more fully integrated, but the beginning of this integration is marked by her publicly sharing a meal with her husband and by the fact that the ceremonial scarf worn on her head during the journey is placed in the granary of the groom's house.

A number of themes in this very typical ritual sequence can be identified and Phylactou considers several of them without giving any one priority. First of all, there is an element of sexual and reproductive symbolism. In the ritual the household of the groom is represented by young men arriving at the bride's house. Similarly, the penetrated household of the bride is not surprisingly represented during the ritual most prominently by the bride herself. Again, the symbolism of the arrow planted in the grain is sexually evocative.

Secondly there is the symbolism of conquest. The fetching of the bride acts out the entry into a bounded territory by a band of triumphant young men with god-like associations who, although Phylactou does not make the point explicitly, seem to represent a royal army who receive tribute from admiring villagers as they proceed on their way to bring back that which will ensure their glorious reproduction. The conquering symbolism comes not only from the groom's party's dances but also from the arrow which the leader of the young men carries prominently and with which in some cases he 'catches' the bride by hooking her by her clothing. In fact the symbolism of the arrow reveals just how complex a totality is invoked in this marriage ritual and introduces yet further themes. Obviously the arrow is a weapon and perhaps a sign of the hunter (Phylactou 1989: 263) but it is also much more and has been very variously interpreted. The arrow is a central symbol, not only in the Tibetan culture area, but throughout the Mahayana Buddhist world, where it often stands for religion illuminating and fertilising the world. In the marriage ritual Phylactou stresses that one of its associations is that of a cosmic tree connecting the gods with the world of humans and so the entry of the young men carrying the arrow can also be seen as the entry of the messenger of the gods into the house which is the centre of human production and reproduction.

Even this multitude of associations does not, however, exhaust the connotations of the symbolism of Ladakhi marriage and we find yet another element that could be repeated from a wide range of ethnographic areas: the symbolism of food and of the wealth of the house, both principally represented by grain. The bride is separated from a number of key parts of the house, including the central post and the main hearth. The central post can also be assimilated to the arrow, which connects the world of the gods with that of humans, and by being forcibly removed from it the bride is as though separated from the fertilising life principle of her own house. Similarly, by being ritually separated from the hearth, the bride is being separated from another area associated with the food-producing centre of the house. It is as if in submitting to the entry of the wife-takers the household is abandoning that which sustains its vitality.

The bride herself is also in many ways associated with wealth and grain. If the groom is represented by the arrow, she must surely be associated with the grain in which the arrow is repeatedly planted. Again, when the bride leaves her natal house her departure is seen as a threat to the wealth of the house in that she takes some of it with her and it is feared she might take more. In a sense the bride comes to be seen as part of the food supply and, more generally, of the fertility of both her natal house and of that which she joins. This is marked when her ceremonial scarf is removed from her head and is placed in her husband's granary. Having arrived in her husband's house the bride becomes part of what the household will need in order to reproduce and therefore be permanent. The wife-givers are therefore not only allowing themselves to be consumed by outsiders in that they take their women but they are also represented as losing other aspects of their vitality: food and wealth. In a similar way the wife-takers gain all these aspects.

We find in this ritual, therefore, a whole range of evocations made into one. There is the kinship and marriage element, the conquest theme, the alimentary theme, the evocation of submission to an external transcendental force leading to the renunciation of innate vitality, the theme of the recovery of an alien vitality from an outside source, and even the cosmogonic element. This is, of course, the same mixture as we found in the analyses of initiation and sacrifice in the earlier chapters.

The image of the bride-takers' party as that of a conquering expedition is particularly common and so is the reference back to a myth of royal conquest which the rituals of marriage are seen as re-enacting. Thus, in a similar manner, in certain parts of Hindu India, far remote from Ladakh, the groom dresses like a king setting out to conquer a foreign country at the head of an army and again the journey refers to a royal myth of conquest (Zeitlyn 1986, chapter 5).

In ancient Rome we find yet another close parallel. There the marriage ritual re-enacted and celebrated the story of the rape of the Sabine women. According to this story, when the original founders of the city discovered themselves without wives and with uncooperative neighbours they invited one of the neighbouring groups, the Sabines, to a great feast. Halfway through the feast the Romans attacked their guests, captured their daughters and married them next morning. It was this heroic deed which was re-enacted at every Roman marriage where the wife-takers acted the Romans and the wife-givers acted the Sabines. The wife-takers were armed and the wife-givers, as if taken unaware, did not have their weapons with them. As is so often the case, marriage is represented as a re-enactment of a successful raid.

Overall, therefore, Ladakhi marriage follows a familiar pattern, the pattern which so obsessed early anthropologists and which they called 'marriage by capture' (McLennan 1865). In this, one side is represented as raiders capturing a woman, in some cases like a hunter capturing his quarry, while the other side is defeated and loses what the victors gain. The frequency of occurrence of such rituals was variously explained either as a leftover of the transition from matriliny to patriliny, or as revealing in unadorned form what was the real basis of male–female relations, or, in the tradition of the anthropologist Radcliffe-Brown, as showing the combination of disjunction and conjunction in marriage. The matter is, however, not as simple as this.

First of all, it is misleading to think of any one marriage as a once-and-for-all event in the life of a social group, whether it be a village, a lineage, or a house. The expedition of the bride-takers in the Ladakhi case is sometimes seen as alluding to an episode in the well-known story of the culture hero's marriage. In the Roman case, the myth of the rape of the Sabine women also alludes to a once-and-for-all event. This, however, cannot be a complete model of what happens either for a Roman family or a Ladakhi household.

A Ladakhi house is envisaged as a social group lasting through time irrespective of the passage of the generations. It is carefully maintained by its members by means of complicated succession and inheritance strategies. This means *inter alia* that it is involved in many marriages through the length of its existence; some of these marriages are the marriages of its women and some the marriages of its men. In the case of marriages of women of the household the house acts as wife-giver; in the case of the marriages of the men of the household the house acts as wife-taker. Thus the same household creates its phenomenological permanence by being both conquered, when it marries its daughters, and conquering, when it marries its sons. The household must sometimes act as the 'outsiders' penetrating the inside of another household and bringing back and absorbing from it that which it needs in order to continue, and sometimes it must act as the 'insiders', ultimately surrendering to outsiders who penetrate it and remove a vital element from it.

If we bring together the taking of brides and the giving of brides, we can see that the implication of the sequence of marriage rituals is even nearer to the general pattern with which this book is concerned than it seemed when it was merely a fact that all marriage rituals use the same sort of symbolism as initiation or sacrifice. This is because submission to the conquest of native vitality, in this case represented by the young women who were born in the

house, is followed by the conquest of external vitality, represented by
incoming brides. This is the pattern of rebounding violence which in this case,
as in the others, creates an apparently supra-biological, transcendental and
immortal existence for a human group.[2]

The rule of incest by which a Ladakhi house must seek spouses beyond itself
if it is to survive means that the marital destiny of the female and male
members of the house is quite different and this inevitably affects the
conceptualisation of gender. In the light of marriage, focused by marriage
rituals, the single unit which the house represents is revealed as potentially
consisting of two different and contrasting elements. The apparent existence
of these two different types of constituents, which comes to the fore in rituals
such as marriage, is like the evocation of dichotomisation which is created in
the other rituals with which we have been concerned. There, it was the
previously undivided person which became represented as made up of two
conflicting elements, whether these were cattle and speech, as among the
Dinka, or pigs and spirits, as among the Orokaiva. In the Ladakhi case the
subject is not one person but the house and the two ritually constructed
constituents of this house can be labelled 'masculinity' and 'femininity'.
Furthermore, we find that these two constituents have many of the
characteristics with which we are familiar from our other examples. In this
division 'femininity', as is often though not always the case (MacCormack and
Strathern 1980), is associated with a vitality that is both productive and
chaotic, and 'masculinity' is associated with the gods and an other-worldly
image of social continuity and order. The house allows itself to be conquered
in its native, vital, feminine side by external masculine/divine beings at the
marriage of the daughter. Subsequently, however, at the marriage of its sons,
itself acting as a divine/male agent, the house recovers fertility in the form of
external women, thereby completing the sequence of rebounding conquest
when it 'consumes' this kind of 'food' in order to bring about its own
reproduction. We are, therefore, back to exactly the pattern which we saw
underlay all the other phenomena discussed so far.

It might well be objected that this formulation is misleading since it is not
households which live in Ladakh but people, and that these people are either
male or female, so that, for them as individuals, the balanced fluctuation of
being conquered and conquering does not occur. After all it is the men who do
the conquering and it is the women who are conquered and not usually the
other way around. According to this point of view there would be no
reciprocity and no returning flow or rebounding violence for any real person.

Although there is some truth in this objection, in that it probably reflects
certain contexts of experience, there is also a sense in which it is very
misleading in that it ignores the subjective entity which the rituals create: the
house as an immortal social agent. The point is that, for the Ladakhi and
many people like them, ideology makes it appear, in a way that is at least
partly convincing, that the active components of society are not people but

houses. Imagining that agency can only be experienced as emanating from single people is a direct product of our ideology of individualism and is, as Dumont has again and again emphasised, totally misleading for the type of societies with which we have been concerned so far (Dumont 1977).

Belonging to a clan for the Orokaiva, or belonging to a lineage among the Romans, or belonging to a house among the Ladakhi is not like joining a social club or even like being a member of a western family. The sociological and legalistic talk of corporations which, until recently, characterised much of the classical discussion of descent groups in anthropology (Fortes 1953) did little to help make this point clear to non-anthropologists since it obscures the real, sometimes physical, way in which this belonging is experienced. For example, many African and Asian peoples say that members of a descent group share the same bones. To say this is not to use a metaphor for closeness; it means exactly what it says in that these people believe that the bones in their body are a part of a greater undifferentiated totality. In cases such as these the body is not experienced as finally bounded by the air around it; it is also continuous with parts of the bodies of people who in modern western ideology would be seen as 'others'.

For the Ladakhi it is the house of which the inhabitants are a part which is thought of as the prime social actor. Sophie Day, another anthropologist working in Ladakh, has pointed out how a Ladakhi house is a model body with the shrine representing the head (Day 1989), and thus the people in it are part of this body, rather as an arm or a leg is part of a body. This type of idea concerning the house is common in many parts of Asia and beyond and has led Lévi-Strauss to talk of such societies as 'sociétés à maison' or house-based societies (Lévi-Strauss 1984: 189–93; Headley 1987: 133–52).

What such *bodyness* implies is that what happens to other members of your household is, to a certain extent, also happening to you irrespective of whether these others are women or men. Because of this the radical disjunction between different people is far from absolute in such societies. In this book we have already seen how individuals may interconnect much more than the ideology of individualism leads us to believe. For example, I pointed out that it is not just the initiates who are hunted and killed in the first part of Orokaiva initiation but also the whole village with them. Even more clearly we have seen how it is the whole village which conquers external vitality when the initiates return. This is so quite literally since, as we saw, all join the initiates' procession and all take part in the triumphal pig hunt which marks that return. Similarly, I pointed out how the same effect of co-participation with the principals occurs in Dinka sacrifice. People who, with our individualistic way of looking, we would describe as onlookers, themselves become possessed as the main drama occurs. In these cases the boundary between the experience of *Ego* and *Alter* is far from absolute.

This has significance when we think of gender in a case such as Ladakh. Because the Ladakhi household is in one sense one person, what happens to any of its members happens to all. This means that all, whether male or female, also participate in the experiences of the marriage of the other gender. Thus, when the Ladakhi household is conquered and penetrated by wife-takers, all its members, whether female or male, are symbolically conquered, penetrated and 'feminised' and, similarly, when the household captures and consumes a bride all its members, whether female or male, conquer, consume and become 'masculinised' and god-like. This fact is what explains the obvious enjoyment of the female participants in a marriage, especially when they are on the side of the bride-takers. It is as part of the conquering house that they identify themselves in the ritual and beyond and thus, for a time at least, they become symbolically male and rejoice in the victory of the male element in the marriage. Similarly, when the household is penetrated by wife-taking 'outsiders', Phylactou tells us how the brothers of the bride weep with her. Then they are largely identified (and seem to identify themselves) with the feminine element which is being lost from the house.

The sequence of wife-giving and wife-taking experienced by the house over time therefore also becomes an oscillation between moments when the house and all its members are predominantly male and messengers of the gods and moments when the house and all its members are predominantly female.

This internal oscillation in the gender identity of the house is acted out in the ritual by the fact that it is men who principally 'represent' the house of the groom and women who principally 'represent' the house of the bride. In this drama it is theatrically suitable that when the house is being penetrated its identity should be evoked by a woman and that the identity of the penetrating house should be represented by triumphant young men; but these ritual actors represent the much more complex and less dichotomised gender fluctuations taking place in all household members. Thus, in the marriage ritual, women and men battle it out, representing the internal gender transformations of the moral person that is the house.

These women and men acting in the ritual are thus like the cattle and speech in the first part of Dinka sacrifice, partial simplifications in dramatic visual contrast of the more complex and fluctuating invisible reality that they represent. The possibility of the house being represented as male, and then female, and then back again is achieved in part by the fact that it can change the actors who 'stand for' it from men to women. This use of gender symbolism represented by male and female actors may also occur in rituals such as initiation or sacrifice, although this was not the case with the particular examples discussed in the two previous chapters. However, a similar effect is produced in Dinka sacrifice by the butchery of the sacrificial animal when its genitals are removed, thereby producing a physical transformation of the dead animal so that it changes from having a male appearance to having a female appearance.

In a number of recent studies on the symbolism of initiation in New Guinea Marilyn Strathern makes a similar point (1988). She stresses that we should not forget that in those societies, like many of the societies I have discussed in this book, all ritual actors, whether men or women, are potentially masculine and feminine, and that rituals bring out fluctuations in this androgynous balance by using simplifications and reductions of the internal components of this complex balance. In New Guinea, and probably to a varying extent everywhere, people experience their relation to others as interpenetrative much more than our individualist ideology recognises and all people, irrespective of gender, experience on certain occasions and to a certain degree what members of the opposite gender typically experience.

It is therefore as misleading to believe that the caricatures which are acted out in ritual are a guide to everyday gender roles as it would be to believe that the confrontations of Everyman with the seven deadly sins represent what life was like in medieval England. I stress this point because, in order fully to understand the parallel between marriage, rituals of marriage, and such practices as initiation or sacrifice, the indirect relation of the experience of exogamy to the rituals of exogamy needs to be appreciated in the same way as we need to appreciate the relation of religious rituals to religious experience.

This point brings us back to Ladakh and to an element of Ladakhi marriage which I have not yet discussed. Earlier I described the marriage ritual as portraying the house of the bride as vanquished. This is not quite accurate. A characteristic of 'marriage by capture' is that it is a mock capture with the connivance of the losers. This is expressed in many details of the ethnography. Even when Ladakhi do not go through the whole elaborate performance discussed above and instead 'steal the bride', and when one would, therefore, expect to find the element of consent totally absent, we find that if the marriage is to be fully successful it is still necessary to obtain some indication of the willingness of the bride's house to the match, if only belatedly. It would, therefore, be more accurate not to view the state of the wife-giving house in the marriage as one of defeat but to say rather, that, in cases such as Ladakhi marriage, the losers submit to and welcome defeat, though this is only after a show of resistance. In other words, the wife-givers accept, with a degree of *schadenfreude*, that they must give up their women. Why this should be now needs to be examined.

The answer which informants from many different parts of the world tend to give to such a question is that they must lose their daughters if they are to reproduce as proper moral human beings. More specifically, their answer takes the form of a discussion of what the effect of incest would be. They argue that if they did not submit to conquest and to the loss of their females they would also not normally be able to expect to conquer foreign wives from outside. They would then have to become parthenogenic if they were to reproduce and everywhere the belief is that the product of such reproduction would be sub-human children, humans not containing that element which makes them more than animals. In other words, it is necessary for the wife-givers to submit to and collude with the conquest of the wife-takers because only in this way will the group produce children who are fully human and not simply animals lacking an immortal, transcendental quality. For such reproduction to be achieved the household and its members must allow themselves to be killed in their internal native feminine element and to lose this to external, god-like predators. This is, of course, also what happens in Orokaiva initiation where adults have to accept the conquest of their children as pigs if their children are not to remain sub-human, that is just like pigs.

By means of the rebounding violence engendered by the observance of the rules of exogamy the Ladakhi house can then reproduce in a human fashion and its children will be proper human beings. Seen in this way the effect of the incest taboo and the idiom of the marriage rituals discussed above reveal themselves as identical in their fundamental logic to the rituals discussed in the previous part of this book. In all these cases the acceptance of the external conquest of native vitality at one moment is rewarded by the right of consumption of external vitality and this consumed and controlled external vitality becomes the means by which earthly life can continue.

This conclusion has a number of implications for controversial issues in anthropology and these can be noted briefly here. First of all it appears that the symbolism of gender and sexuality, which is so prominent in much religious ritual, cannot be understood properly if we see it as though it was concerned only with the relations between men and women. Rather it should be understood as being used in rituals in an *ad hoc* manner to act out a more fundamental and central logic concerning the establishment of a form of human life which has apparently escaped the biological constraint of death. The demonstration of this point arises from the fact that we have seen how the conjunction and disjunction between humans and animals can be used to exactly the same ends in ritual as the conjunction and disjunction between female and male.

Here the example of the Orokaiva is once again instructive. The Orokaiva are very unusual for New Guinea and Melanesia in that boys and girls are initiated together and in a roughly similar manner. Probably because of this, the opposition between male and female is hardly developed symbolically in the initiation ritual, the burden of representing rebounding violence being almost exclusively carried by animal symbolism and its antithesis, the spirits. But if we were to look elsewhere in New Guinea, to such examples as the Gimi, studied by G. Gillison, we would find that the task of representing rebounding violence is, in their case, carried almost exclusively by gender symbolism. The Gimi ethnography could, therefore, easily have been used to demonstrate my general argument and Gillison's analysis comes very close to the one proposed in this book, but had we done this with this particular example, we would have been in danger of seeing the whole issue simply in gender terms (Gillison 1980). Instead, it should now be apparent that, in New Guinea or elsewhere, gender and animality are alternative symbolic resources which, together or separately, can be used in the processes of rebounding violence which create the transcendental. It is this which is the real basis of the phenomena we have examined, while the symbolic use of ritually constructed differences between animals and humans or female and male are secondary.

Of course, this is not to say that there is no relationship between the social status of women and men and the way masculinity and feminity are used in ritual. It is no accident that it is usually women who are given the role of representing the expelled and consumed entity, the pig-role of Orokaiva symbolism, and that it is the men who are given the conquering 'spirit' role. But even here things are not always predictable. For example, among the Garo, a Himalayan society where recruitment to social groups is matrilineal, but where nonetheless women are fairly powerless, we find a marriage ritual which is strikingly reminiscent of the Ladakhi one but where it is the groom who is captured and conquered and the family of the bride who do the conquering (Burling 1963: 83 ff.). However, even in this case we should not forget that it is the *men* of the family of the bride who do the conquering.

Another general implication of the conclusion that marriage rituals and such rituals as sacrifice and initiations are simply different manifestations of an underlying pattern concerns anthropological theories of incest. In the light of the above it would appear that the incest taboo too, in so far as it implies submission to a conquest by outsiders of a native element which is recompensed by the promise of the recovery of that element in a conquered form from an outside source, is just one among several mechanisms, including sacrifice and initiation, which all do the same thing. That is, they transform the fluidity of human life in such a way that it may appear governed by eternal institutional and cognitive structures. After all, the statements of informants concerning the consequences of incest are precisely that the rules are necessary if society is not to be overturned in its most fundamental aspect and if humans are to be truly differentiated from animals. In this perspective, obedience to the rules of incest and exogamy would be a kind of unfocused sacrifice, where members of a social group submit to almost killing a side of themselves associated with uncontrolled vitality in order that an eternal death-defying element might emerge, which would then have the right to conquer vitality from outside. Once again, this vitality differs from that which has been abandoned in that it is totally subordinated to the transcendental element which has been constructed by the renunciation.

There are, however, also some differences between the sequence of rebounding violence as it is acted out in marriage rituals and the other examples discussed in this book, although these are more a matter of degree than differences in kind. The fact that the same unit is simultaneously conquered and conqueror means that the sequencing that we saw in Orokaiva initiation or in Buid sacrifice is not so clearly present in a temporal sequence. In these rituals the first violence or conquest clearly precedes the rebounding violence, while in the marriage of ordinary people in Ladakh there is no reason why a house should be first conquered and then conquering. It could just as well be the other way round. Two points should, however, qualify such a distinction. Firstly, even for a case such as Orokaiva initiation we noted how the ritual is not a once-and-for-all affair. As Iteanu stresses, this ritual shares a similar form to rituals such as marriage or funerals. It is, therefore, part of a long chain with no necessary beginning or end. This is all the more so because, as we saw, people do not just participate in their own initiation but they also participate in repeated initiations at which they vicariously re-experience the transformation from prey into hunter.

The second reason why the difference in the sequencing of rebounding conquest in initiation and marriage is not so great as might appear at first concerns the fact that it is possible for marriage to take on a unidirectional character, which becomes the basis of a legitimised state hierarchy (Friedman and Rowlands 1977). Then, the symbolism of the reconquest of the vital becomes once again open-ended and can thus, in suitable circumstances, be expanded so as to become a general idiom of militarism, expansion and domination. In just the same way as in the Indian and Japanese cases when we move from the formulation of rebounding violence of ordinary people to that of the state we find that the aggressive unidirectional potential ot the symbolism comes to the fore and that this can be expressed in the idiom of marriage as easily as it is in Hinduism in the idiom of sacrifice.

Indeed, this element of absolute conquest is found in the organisation of marriage in some of the social systems which have already been considered in this chapter, and here again Ladakh can serve as an example. If, from the point of view of a particular house, the marriage of males and females occurs equally frequently and is monogamous, then the experiences of conquest and of being conquered cancel each other out. However, matters are not so simple. The whole Tibetan culture area is famous in the literature as a society where the, by now, largely obsolete practice of polyandry occurred. Polyandry is the practice whereby a number of men, usually brothers, marry a single wife. In fact, side by side with polyandry, there also existed in Ladakh the practice of polygamy in which one man marries a number of wives. The presence of these possibilities, side by side with the widespread possibility of monogamy, can only be understood in relation to each other and together with the degree of social inequality which existed in the past in that part of the world. Although Ladakhi marriage is thought of as an alliance between equals, the overall distribution of marriages implied the very opposite of equality. By and large the rich and powerful, kings for example, would take many wives, while the subject houses were much more likely to opt for polyandry or monogamy.

What this meant was that the kings would find themselves much more often in the position of wife-taking conquerors and much less often in the position of wife-giving conquered, while the reverse would apply to those of inferior status. This symbolical asymmetric conquest was, of course, not all there was to the distinction between different social ranks. The marriage imbalance meant, however, that the rich and powerful were by their marriage strategy repeatedly conquering and using their conquered vitality to reproduce themselves, while the inferiors, on the other hand, could only adopt the role of divine conquerors and be revitalised by means of the absorption of external women less frequently.

We are, therefore, back with the third potential political manifestation of the symbolism of rebounding violence touched on in the previous chapter. The first possibility examined was a matter of the symbolic construction of a permanent order of balanced reproduction; the second was the turning of the final conquest outward so that it became an idiom of military expansion. In the third, the same aggressive element as in the second possibility is not turned towards outsiders but towards insiders of lower status, thus producing an ideology of social ranking.

In order to make this point more fully and to go more deeply into the political implications of the use of the marriage form of rebounding conquest for expressing domination within one political unit I turn to yet another different ethnographic example. This example is found in David Lan's powerful study of Shona spirit mediums and of their relation to the guerrillas who liberated Zimbabwe (Lan 1985). Much of the material discussed by Lan is reminiscent of that from Ladakh and ancient Rome in so far as it concerns marriage. Every Shona marriage refers back to an origin myth concerning the conquest of the land where the present-day owners have established their kingdoms. In the case discussed by Lan, this is the conquest of the Dande valley by the Korekore Shona. The predominantly male ancestors of the Korekore are believed to have gained the land by their victory over aboriginal peoples who previously owned it. But, according to the myth, not only did the ancestors defeat and kill the aborigines, they also forcibly married their women so that, as in the case of the Romans and the Sabines, a hierarchical alliance was formed which led to the production of progeny.

In referring back to this origin myth the Shona therefore represent marriage as a matter of conquest by the wife-takers. But that is not all: the wife-givers are also seen as 'life-givers' and that is what they are called. The wives whom the wife-givers supply are shown in this way to be as essential for reproduction as the husbands. Like the pigs of the Orokaiva the wives are the suppliers of a vitality which must be conquered and ordered in order to become legitimate.

The life given by the 'life-givers' takes many forms, all of which in some ways refer to water and wetness. To understand the full significance of this wetness we once again need to understand the ritual constituents of the person. For the Shona small children are all soft flesh and blood which comes from the mother. At first they are without any hard bones, but as they grow up the hard stuff develops inside them. This can be seen particularly when the teeth pierce the gums of babies and when their fontanelle closes up (Lan 1985: 93). The hard stuff comes from the father and ultimately the ancestors. In a sense, as the hard stuff increases the ancestors are taking over. Thus, the soft stuff, which comes from the mother, is gradually defeated in life, but only after the reproductive period of humans is passed. It is, therefore, not surprising that the defeated aborigines who supplied the ancestors with wives and the Korekore with mothers should be associated with life-giving wet stuff in the form of blood.

This is not all, however. The aborigines did not just give blood, they also gave the water which produces the food the body needs to consume in order to live. We find, therefore, in Shona mythology the idea that, just as the aborigines gave wet children to their husbands/conquerors in the past, these aboriginals still now provide the ultimate mystical source of the life-giving wetness on which their descendants rely: they give rain to their matrilineal descendants.

All these themes could probably be understood in Ladakh or, at least, in those parts of Tibet where similar ideas are found,[3] but a number of other aspects of Shona affinity would be less familiar. Because Shona chiefs and chiefly lineages stand in a relation of wife-takers to the lineages of many of their subjects, the present-day relation between affines is merged and expressed in the idiom of political and military subordination. This means that, unlike Ladakh where marriage is principally thought of as an alliance between equals, the idiom of Shona marriage can carry with it an image of non-reciprocity, something found in many other parts of the world.

Of course the lineages of chiefs also produce female children and therefore these lineages are also caught in the reciprocal cycles of being conquered internally through their women and conquering women externally. But Shona marriage also always implies the possibility of unidirectional exchange. Irrespective of what might happen in individual cases, chiefdoms are visualised as being dominated by a royal descent group, which takes wives from other subject descent groups, but does not, in terms of the political imagery, give wives back to these lower groups. This mixture of the reproductive reciprocal model with the hierarchical unidirectional model might seem muddling but, in fact, it is typical. The expansionist implications of rebounding violence are seen in all the examples we have examined and are, as here, merely a variant of the reproductive mode.

The full significance of this merging lies in the fact that this is what gives expansion or, as here, hierarchy its legitimacy and power, since to refuse it can appear as coming close to refusing reproduction itself.

In terms of Shona political imagery the members of royal lineages of the chiefs are therefore principally thought of as wife-takers of their subjects, who cannot normally be also represented as being, at other moments, wife-givers to their subjects, because this would imply subjection. This does not, however, mean that the chiefs are any the less caught in a chain of rebounding violence than anybody else. It means that as far as politics is concerned for them the chain of rebounding violence is represented differently. For chiefs the right to take wives and thereby perhaps make subjects out of their families is the rebound of the chiefs allowing themselves to be willingly conquered, not by wife-takers, but by their ancestors.

We saw how for the Shona growing old is a matter of the hard ancestral bone vanquishing the feminine, vital, wet, blood element in the person. This ancestral drying is a sign both of the fact that the living are on the way to becoming ancestors themselves and of their total and willing surrender to the duty which the ancestors require of them. Submission to the ancestor's authority is the guarantee of a successful moral life. In the case of a chief, if he submits to the will of his ancestors, that is if he allows himself to become an ancestor, he will have many subjects, many wife-givers and many children.

In terms of the pattern of rebounding violence we can see that the chief's conquest of external, wet-giving life-givers is the reward for his willing surrender of his native vitality to the ancestors through drying and through the surrender of his individual will. This submission to the conquest of the ancestors takes on a very specific form at certain critical moments. The Shona believe that the disembodied spirits of dead chiefs return in the body of living spirit mediums, and through the mouths of the mediums the ancestors give their orders to the living chiefs. If the living chiefs submit to the wishes of their ancestors, that is to an internal penetration which leads to the drying of the body and ultimately to death and rebirth in the bodies of mediums, then and only then will their subjects in their turn be willingly conquered by the chief's legitimate rule. This is seen to occur in a way that is similar to that of a son conquered by his father and to the wife-givers being consumed as they 'give life' to the wife-takers.

But the converse is also true. If a chief is believed to refuse the conquest of his ancestors and to disobey the wishes they convey via the mediums, then his subjects (wife-givers) should refuse to give up their vitality to him, since he has refused to be legitimately conquered himself.

This is exactly what happened at the beginning of the final successful phase of the war of liberation against the Rhodesian government, when guerrillas began to enter Zimbabwe through Dande. Many of the traditional Korekore chiefs of Dande were believed by their subjects to have 'sold out' to the whites during the colonial period. This 'selling out' was understood by their subjects as the chiefs failing the ancestors' supreme order to their descendants that they should take care of the land, the central patrimony which was in their trust. Because the chiefs were disobeying the ancestors in this way, their spirits, speaking through the mouths of the mediums, withdrew their protection and guidance from the chiefs and thereby delegitimised their rule.

On the other hand, in the persons of the newly arrived guerrillas the mediums were offered alternative descendants. These were not descendants because of biological kinship, but, in so far as the guerrillas declared themselves the restorers of the land, they became descendants as a result of obedience. Many mediums therefore recognised the guerrillas as alternatives to the chiefs who had broken with the ancestors and who had therefore lost their support. By making the guerrillas a kind of chief, the spirits of the ancestors bestowed on these young men the legitimate right to conquer the people by requiring them to obey and submit to these new chiefly 'descendants', since these descendants were in their turn obeying their ancestors. In other words the guerrillas were substituted for the failed chiefs in the chain of rebounding violence.

For their part, the guerrillas saw that, if they were to win the confidence of the people, they had to recognise the authority of the mediums and they therefore accepted the conquest of the ancestors by their obedience to certain rules specified by the mediums and by their participation in the ancestral rituals. This was no mere cynical manipulation of the peasants; it was a genuine and inevitable process of harmonisation of their experiences and desires with those of the people with whom they were interacting on a daily basis and on whom they relied for their safety. They thus became, for a while at least, the true children of the ancestral chiefs, and in return for being conquered, they were promised conquest of the fertility of the land, the subjects, affines, the old chiefs, and ultimately their enemies. The guerrillas had become the legitimate leaders of the people with the right to compel the unwilling.

This Shona example, as analysed by Lan, whom I have followed entirely here, confirms how the idiom of rebounding violence, sometimes found in ideas surrounding marriage, is continuous with the idiom of rebounding violence revealed in rituals concerned with the conquest of a living generation by an antecedent one. The conquest of the chiefs by their ancestral spirits in the ritual of spirit possession, something which is similar in form to what happens in Orokaiva initiation, leads directly to the politically significant conquest by the chief of his 'wife-giving life-giving' subjects. Furthermore, as in all the other cases we have seen, the chain of rebounding violence can lead to an expansionist idiom of the conquest of others, who in future may become new wife-givers and new subjects.

However, the case analysed by Lan reveals yet another aspect of the political implications of this theme. However oppressive the action of the people concerned in all the systems we have looked at may seem, they at least imply an organic link between conquerors and conquered. Even though the subjects in a Shona chiefdom are conquered by their chiefs they are still 'life-givers' to him, and they too, given the logic of rebounding violence, are promised future consuming conquests, even though these might be only of their children or sacrificial animals. However, when rulers such as Shona chiefs choose to retain their domination, but refuse the legitimation of rebounding conquest because they refuse to be conquered by their ancestors, then they remove themselves from the organic chain and their rule is revealed as unadorned exploitation and subjects will seek the earliest opportunity to revolt against their dominators.[4] The idiom of rebounding violence is thus revealed to lie at the back of some of the more holistic forms of political subordination, but it is also clear that there are other forms of political exploitation in which the rulers seek to escape from the limits of the model.

6

Millenarianism

In the previous five chapters I have been concerned to give a detailed description of the symbolism of rituals which construct rebounding violence. In focusing on the coherence of this structure across different cultural systems, I may have given the misleading impression that the system is itself without tensions and strains. In fact, the truth is very different. These phantasmagoric corporate institutions do not create their claims to permanence and immortality without an effort and conflict which is itself often a violent one. Rituals are not always straightforward and convincing to all their participants; nor are the sociological results of these rituals of authority and of aggression easily predictable.

The purpose of this chapter and the next is to correct this impression of over-coherence. When we look at the rituals more from the point of view of the individuals concerned and from the point of view of their own experience, or when we consider the history of specific political systems at specific moments, it becomes clear that the process does not necessarily go smoothly or predictably. In ritual, in fact, the meanings conjured up are always on the point of faltering.

The study of public rituals does not normally enable the anthropologist to record such experiential uncertainty. There are two main reasons for this. First, anthropologists usually feel that they have enough on their hands recording and interpreting the main thrust of the proceedings without also having to cope with the finer nuances expressed in the behaviour of individuals. Secondly, rituals are occasions on which such individual doubts are not usually in evidence since, in ritual, the behaviour of the participants is as if orchestrated by a shared score. Furthermore, the formalisation of ritual speech, song and action itself makes individual expression of dissent very difficult to express within the medium (Bloch 1974).

There are, however, occasions when the conditions of life are so obviously troublesome that individual doubts join together and emerge into the open, leading to fundamental and dramatic changes in the rituals and in the images they evoke. In order to show the effect of such a situation on the symbolism of

rebounding violence I turn first to some aspects of the history and
anthropology of central Madagascar.

In this book I have deliberately avoided discussing the ethnography of the
Merina of Madagascar because, as was noted in the first chapter, this book is
in part an attempt to see whether some of the conclusions I drew in a study of
the Merina circumcision ceremony could be applied more widely to different
parts of the world. At this point, however, it is convenient to turn briefly to the
Merina and their circumcision ceremony and at the same time to remind the
reader of some of the cases already discussed in order to introduce a
consideration of the effect of political circumstances on the much more well-
known case: that of Jewish circumcision at the time when Christianity was just
beginning to be established.

In a way which is somewhat similar to the Shona the Merina represent
people in rituals as made up of two elements: an ancestral, permanent, dry
element and a vital, chaotic, wet element. The wet is represented as
dominating in the newly born child, but as the child proceeds through life the
wet element gradually gives way to the dry element. The wet element only
disappears completely, however, some time after death when the corpse,
which has previously been temporarily buried in order to 'dry', is exhumed
and placed in a shared monumental tomb. This dry element is uniquely human
and its growth in the person signifies the increasing connection with the
ancestors and the descent group. Thus, throughout life, a person gradually
becomes an ancestor and a member of a permanent descent group. However,
as is the case for the Orokaiva, while he or she is still alive a person is never
completely an ancestor or completely a member of a life-transcending descent
group. This is because a live person is by definition also vital and therefore also
partly wet.

The wet element, unlike the dry element, is common to all forms of life. It is
associated with sensuous enjoyment and individual practical activity; it
implies involvement in such dialectical processes of change as birth, sexuality
and death. Unlike the dry, ancestral element which should remain in a fixed
quantity within the descent group, the wet element flows and changes like the
vitality it represents.

In the Merina circumcision ritual the wet and dry elements in the body are
represented in a number of ways which are reminiscent of some of the other
examples already discussed in this book. For example the wet vitality is
represented at certain moments of the ritual by plants and animals which are
seen as either particularly strong or particularly fertile. At other moments wet
vitality is represented by women, who contrast in their ritual role with men,
who depict the dry ancestral component. It should be remembered, however,
that, as in the case of Ladakh, this use of gender is largely to signify a
dichotomy which is not primarily concerned with gender, and that these are
ritual roles which men and women take on. Although the Merina seem to
believe that on balance the vital wet element is more prominent in women than

in men, they are also well aware that, outside the drama of ritual, things are more ambiguous; since both men and women are alive and both will eventually die, both partake of the wet vital quality and both will in the end become completely dry ancestors.[1]

The ritual proceeds in a way that will by now be familiar to the reader of this book. The Merina circumcision begins with the increasing polarisation of the two contradictory wet and dry elements through a process of dramatic contrast which was called by Bateson in *Naven* schismogenesis (Bateson 1958: 178).[2] This schismogenesis has, as Bateson himself noted and as we saw in the Dinka case, two sides. It has a public side in which material symbols representing the two elements are dramatically opposed in the ritual and a hidden, experiential, internal side which for the participants seems to occur inside their body as an internal refraction of what happens 'on stage'.

Once the opposition between the two elements has been evoked these elements are then represented as engaged in an uneven conflict in which the ancestral conquers and expels the vital. This conquest corresponds to the victory of the bird-like spirits over the pig-like children in the first part of Orokaiva initiation or the victory of speech over cattle in Dinka sacrifice. In Merina circumcision the struggle and the ultimate victory of the first conquest is manifested by attacks on plants and women and culminates in the suggested 'almost killing' of the feminine aspect of the child by the operation itself.

But then, as in the other rituals we have considered, the act of violence is followed by a rebounding violence in the final part of the ritual. The child, having symbolically died and become all 'dry' like an ancestor, recovers the wet vital element by the conquest and consumption of the vitality of beings external to himself. This second conquest takes the form of an allusion to the sexual conquest of women by men and of the dramatically violent consumption of particularly vital and fertile animals and plants during a mock physical struggle (Bloch 1986: 72).

For a period during the nineteenth century this ritual, which previously had merely been a family or descent group ritual, became a great state ritual. This occurred when, as a result of complex political and economic circumstances, the Merina state expanded into an aggressive, growing empire which conquered nearly the whole of Madagascar. This dramatic growth was accompanied by the development of a state religion cobbled together from various traditional and imported elements, chief among which was the circumcision ritual. As a result the circumcision ritual became a great state ritual focused on the circumcision of royal princes.

These state circumcisions were occasions when the whole kingdom, led by the monarch, participated in the process of rebounding violence. Because, as we have seen, the boundary between the main participants and other people is weak during ritual, the ritual conquest of natural vitality of and by the circumcised became a conquest of and by the whole kingdom. All submitted to conquest by the ancestors in unison with the initiates and all then participated in the reconquest of external vitality. But, just as in the Japanese and Hindu examples, transposing the symbolism of rebounding violence to the level of the state gave a different emphasis to the concluding reconquest of external vitality. Firstly, this reconquest of external vitality by the royal child and, by implication, by the royal family took on an element of the symbolic conquest of subjects by the monarch. This part of the ritual represents the conquest and consumption of the vitality of youth by the dryness of the ancestors. The king therefore appeared in the ritual as a sort of ancestor conquering his over-vital children and thereby legitimating his power over his subjects in a way reminiscent of the Shona case.

Secondly, when the Merina were militarily strong, as was the case during the first part of the nineteenth century, the ritual ended with the kind of aggression against neighbours that we saw suggested in the Orokaiva ritual, since in the Merina case neighbours also became associated with the representatives of external vitality in the ritual so that they too needed to be vanquished and consumed. State-wide circumcision rituals therefore culminated naturally in grandiose, aggressive, military parades. Moreover, on occasion these parades were the beginning of real military expeditions, involving tens of thousands of people carrying British-made rifles and leading to horrifying carnage, rape, pillaging and the taking of slaves (Bloch 1986).

Things did not, however, always go well for the Merina and at certain times this state of affairs led, as among the Shona, to the legitimation of the ruler being refused by the subjects. This is what happened in the year 1863 when the king of the moment, Radama II, was, amid great economic and political turmoil, believed by many Merina to have abandoned the country to foreigners, mainly the French and the British, who had been trying by various means to gain religious, ideological, commercial and military footholds on the island.

One aspect of this supposed abdication to outsiders was that Radama II had abolished state rituals such as the state circumcision ritual. The reaction to this situation was a dramatic religious revolt which took place at a time when the royal circumcision ritual could have been expected to occur. All over the country people abandoned their agricultural tasks and left their families as they became possessed by the ancestors and especially by dead rulers. Then they advanced in great processions towards the capital, acting as though they were carrying the luggage of the dead kings and queens and as though they were about to reinstall these dead rulers in the royal palace. On their way towards the capital the possessed performed the opening parts of various rituals which had been abandoned by Radama II, above all the ritual of circumcision (Bloch 1986: 145ff.). The ultimate result of this movement was general chaos which led to the killing of Radama II and the establishment of a very different political system.

This popular and spontaneous reaction is quite understandable in terms of Merina symbolism if we look at it in the light of rebounding violence.

Ordinary people felt that the situation brought about by Radama II's rule implied disordered chaos and that the abandonment of the rituals was tantamount to the refusal to summon back the ancestral order which would end that chaos, and which would have been achieved in the first part of the ritual of circumcision. Radama was seen as having refused submission to the conquest of the ancestors and as having submitted instead to conquest by predatory outsiders. These outsiders would by definition consider the Merina as a different species and hence could never lead them to become the rebounding conquerors of external vitality. Instead, the Merina feared, they would be treated like the plants in their own circumcision ritual or the pigs in Orokaiva initiation; that is, they would themselves be ritually consumed to provide vitality for the foreigner.

So the people began the ritual inside their own bodies and, as they felt the ancestors rise up and submitted to this internal first conquest, they became possessed. In doing this they were reversing the process of refraction of ritual where the symbolic acts create an internal state, such as occurs when Dinka onlookers become possessed as a result of the weakening of the cattle on the ceremonial ground. By becoming possessed the Merina were acting as though the internal sensation of possession were to be the cause and start of the performance of the abandoned ritual.

And so the possessed Merina began to carry out the first part of the ritual of circumcision on their own initiative. It was as if they were trying to take the whole country with them in the first conquest, as would have occurred in the royal circumcision rituals, to bring back the whole country under the rule of the ancestors, in the way the ancestors invade the initiates, dry them and make them, for a moment, ancestors themselves. But they were doing this without the leadership of earthly instituted authorities and so they had to substitute dead rulers as replacements for the unsatisfactory live one.

So the Merina of 1863, as they abandoned earthly productive activities and became possessed and as they then spontaneously began the ritual of circumcision, were re-enacting the symbolical death of the first conquest as they submitted to the will of their ancestors. But they were doing this in defiance of the currently instituted political authorities. This contrasts with most of the cases discussed so far with the exception of the Shona example. In these other cases the sequence of rebounding conquest legitimates instituted authority; in this case it undermined it. It is, therefore, particularly important to see how what the Merina rebels were doing differed in terms of rebounding violence from the symbolic practice of cases such as Orokaiva sacrifice or Japanese religion.

The difference lies in the fact that, although the Merina possessed were willingly submitting to the first conquest, they were not going on to the second rebounding conquest. This would have involved the reconsumption of the vital from an external source and this is the way by which the participants recover life and re-establish society regulated by the ancestors' representatives in the normal ritual, a recovery which in the Merina circumcision ceremony begins with the actual operation and culminates in the symbolic consumption of plants and women. By carrying out only the first part of the ritual they were willingly going beyond life as they gave up their natal vitality through possession and became ancestors under the rule of ancestral kings but they were not then returning to vitality through the mediation of consumption and rebounding violence. It was as if the Buid, having flown off in spirit on the back of their spirit familiars, had not then returned to earth and had remained suspended there above the world of the living, or as if the Orokaiva initiates had remained for ever as spirits in the dark in the forest.

This intention to leave the world of the living and never to come back explains the significance of the abandonment of agricultural tasks, especially forward-looking agricultural tasks such as irrigating, sowing and transplanting. For the possessed Merina were in fact refusing reproduction altogether, in all its forms, and exchanging reproductivity for the unchanging, other-worldly permanence of ancestorhood and the tomb. They were not intending to consume the vital and thus gain strength, since they did not want to submit to living rulers who had failed them. Instead, they wanted to establish the kingdom of the dead, of the ancestors, a kingdom which was eternal because it was on the other side of death. The first part of rebounding conquest which symbolically so often takes the form of a funeral, as is the case for the first part of Orokaiva initiation, was thus particularly suitable for their purpose, so long as it was not followed by the second part of the ritual.

I have quite deliberately worded my description here so as to recall the extensive literature on what anthropologists have come to call 'millenarian movements'. Originally, of course, this term applied to medieval Christian movements which arose particularly during times of uncertainty, and in which the participants acted to hasten the end of the world in order to exchange it for an eternal life beyond the grave. Those who were swept up in the religious fervour which characterised the most intense phases of these movements also abandoned normal day-to-day reproductive activity, whether sexual or economic. They welcomed the prospect of the millennium because they believed that a period of chaos and destruction would only be a prelude to the second coming of Christ. Their behaviour was designed to show that it was the kingdom of Christ on earth which they were awaiting, that they expected nothing further from ordinary, earthly life and did not look to participate in its pleasures or necessities. At the second coming, every human soul would be judged at once and the righteous would inherit a world without change and time (Lanternari 1963). Symbolically, therefore, the millennium would be the occasion of a world-wide funeral which all should welcome as it would herald a rebirth in another non-vital and immortal existence. This is exactly what the Merina rebels of 1863 wanted in their very different terms and what they were hoping to bring about by an unconditional submission to the ancestors.

The key elements of millenarian movements, whether Christian or not, seem to lie precisely in this refusal of the second phase of rebounding violence, that is, a refusal of the conquest of external vitality which is therefore ultimately a refusal to continue with earthly life. When matters are beyond practical remedy, the remedy is to hasten the end of the practical. This is a state of affairs already touched on in this book; after all this is exactly what the African diviner advises when he suggests to the patient that, since the first attempt to expel disease has failed, the patient should instead join the disease, turn against himself and organise his own funeral as in Dinka sacrifice. But unlike the type of sacrifice so far discussed, millenarianism stops at this initial stage.

This explains why the Merina rebels were only interested in the first part of the circumcision ritual, the part which is a funeral, and not in the part which glorifies violent consumption. It also explains why such a movement is a challenge to earthly authorities. The second part of the ritual places, or rather sandwiches, the establishment of authority between the revival brought about by the consumption of external vitality and its expansion into aggression. But if the participants prefer to halt the ritual at the point where they are themselves conquered and as if dead, rejecting the consumption of external vitality which will ritually revitalise them, then there will be no final outwardly directed act of conquest, and no legitimation for earthly authority.

Indeed there is nothing more characteristic of millenarian movements than their refusal of reproduction, which in the Merina case took the form of the abandonment of agricultural tasks. The true proof of the devotee, whether in medieval Europe or in modern Melanesia (Burridge 1969) in what have been called cargo cults, is the refusal to engage in such activities as sowing for the next harvest and producing children, since to continue earthly life would belie the commitment to total universal earthly death.

That aspect of millenarianism which makes it refuse the second part of rebounding conquest throws light on an unexpected and much discussed aspect of early Christianity: the attitude of Paul and the early church to the same matter that concerned the Merina rebels of the nineteenth century, namely circumcision.

It has been a commonplace among social scientists to argue that Christianity had many of the elements of a millenarian movement especially because of the early Christian's expectation of the imminent second coming of Christ, a second coming which was to mark the end of practical daily life (e.g. Kautsky 1953). Most of these writers see Christianity as a kind of revolutionary response to Roman colonialism, although it is clear that, as in the Merina case, the early Christians were much more concerned with the political and religious failure of their own leaders in the face of the ideological onslaught of Rome than with the Romans themselves. Put in its usual terms, this sort of assertion about Christianity always in fact remains somewhat vague, but if we turn in detail to the subject of circumcision we find that the characteristic features of millenarian thought as we have been describing it appear in a much more precise and diagnostic way.

The epistles of Paul, or at least some of them, are the earliest Christian documents in the Bible. They are largely devoted to the setting up of churches in the eastern Roman world but it is also clear that these churches were not expected to last long as Paul and the early Christians were expecting that Christ would come again and end the earthly world in their lifetime. Thus, in the first epistle to the Corinthians, Paul expresses himself in ways that would have been familiar to the Merina rebels or to any cargo cultist: 'our time is growing short. Those who have wives should live as though they had none . . . I say this because the world as we know it is passing away' (7.29–31). 'After that will come the end, when he [Christ] hands over the kingdom to God the Father, having done away with every sovereignty, authority, and power' (15.25–25).[3]

The theology of the Pauline epistles is dominated by the emphasis on the crucifixion and they contain no mention of the virgin birth. Above all, Paul was asking the early Christians to join in Christ's death in the hope of a communal resurrection in an immortal form: 'flesh and blood cannot inherit the kingdom of God and the perishable cannot inherit what lasts for ever. I will tell you something that has been secret: that we are not all going to die, but we shall all be changed' (15.51). This is not surprising since all millenarianism always looks forward to death to end it all, not an individual death, however, but a communal death which will bring an end to all forms of practical process in human life and replace failed earthly leaders with incorruptible transcendental ones.

However, and this has struck many people as odd, considerable space in the epistles is also devoted to a controversy among early Christians over whether non-Jewish converts would have to be circumcised at the same time as they were baptised. This is part of Paul's general insistence on the irrelevance of Jewish law, which had previously been seen as the main guide to holiness. Unlike some other early Christians Paul seems to have been against compulsory circumcision for converts (Armstrong 1983: 82–7). The explanation usually given for the Pauline attitude is the fact that he was the champion of the universality of Christianity and that he wanted to make it easy for Gentiles to convert. Of course there can be no doubt that this universalism was central for Paul, but I find this argument quite insufficient to explain the particular prominence given to the issue of circumcision. After all, it it not all that much to ask of new converts and, furthermore, circumcision never seems to have been an obstacle to the universalist appeal of Islam.

On the other hand, the parallel with the Merina case suggests another more fundamental reason, which fits in well with the tenor of the epistles in their emphasis on Christ's death and resurrection. The Merina rebels felt they were joining their ancestors and so they became possessed. In doing this they were following the symbolism of the first part of their rituals which involves a move out of transformative life to a permanent existence as a dry ancestor. The first part of the Merina circumcision ritual is thus like a funeral following a willingly experienced symbolic death. This was normally followed by a conquering return to life under the order of the ancestors. The rebels, however, as we saw, did not want to go on to return to vitality via consumption of either food or women since they had given up earthly existence, but they hoped, rather, for a permanent continuation of their lives beyond perishable flesh and bone. It would seem that just the same experience underlies Paul's attitude.

In order to understand what the rejection of the need for circumcision might mean it is obviously essential to understand what circumcision meant for those who practised it. On this the Bible is very clear. For the ancient Jews circumcision was one form of the covenant between man and God (Genesis 17). The covenant itself was envisaged totally within the framework of rebounding conquest as we have already seen in the discussion of Abraham's sacrifice of Isaac. The promise of the Old Testament was that, if the ancient Jews totally submitted to God to the extent that they were willing to be killed by God if He so wished, they would then be rewarded by a fruitful life and even the conquest of their enemies. The life so obtained, like life after Orokaiva initiation, would be abundant so long as the recipients marked their permanent submission to the conquest by God by allowing Him to regulate the most fundamental aspects of their bodily functions, such as eating according to His laws and bearing His scar on their genitals.

Circumcision is, thus, first of all a willingness to submit to the conquest of God and, as in the story of Abraham and Isaac, to co-operate with His apparently murderous intentions. This is made particularly clear in an alternative origin story for circumcision given in the Bible (Exodus 4.24–26). Yahweh, having had a fair amount of trouble making Moses obey, attempts to kill him and/or his son for no clear reason when they are on their way to Egypt. However, death is once again avoided at the last moment through the intervention of Moses's wife who circumcises them both. Circumcision appears here as a last-moment alternative to, or perhaps postponement of, death which is granted precisely because of the actors' willing submission to conquest.

But then this willing submission and movement towards death becomes in these stories, as in ritual, the prelude to reproduction, that is earthly sexual reproduction marked by a quasi-mortal wound inflicted in obedience to God's will. The circumcised penis was the sign of willingness to submit to and be conquered by God even to the point of death or pseudo-death. Just as in ritual, the logic of rebounding violence determined that this submission was followed by a return to a successful mastery of the world, in this case through a most explicitly sanctified reproductivity. Thus God promises Abraham as a benefit of the covenant of circumcision 'I will make you father of a multitude of nations. I will make you most fruitful' (Genesis 17.5–6). 'I will give to you and your descendants after you the land you are living in, the whole land of Canaan' (Genesis 17.8).

The lack of insistence on circumcision by Paul seems to relate precisely to these political and reproductive aspects of the practice. As Paul was expecting the imminent second coming of Christ and of the last judgment, his refusal of the need for circumcision and of other laws intended to regulate continuing earthly existence was part of the general millenarian tenor of much of his Christianity.

In this perspective the insistence on a practice concerned with the continuation of reproduction, holy or otherwise, must have seemed a manifestation of lack of faith in the second coming and Paul's opposition, or at least indifference, to circumcision is easily understood. It seems to be one part of a more general refusal of reproduction which also largely explains Paul's famous ambivalence towards marriage and towards women. This is because femininity stands for earthly process in the antithetical symbolism of Judaeo-Christian religious symbolism in a way that is somewhat similar to its role in Merina ritual symbolism.

Paul was therefore opposed to the following of Jewish law on circumcision and on other matters, not principally because he was a universalist, but because these laws were a matter of continuing earthly life informed by the God-inflicted wound and he wanted to end earthly life. He wanted the Christians to join in Christ's death to the extent that life 'as we know it' would end.

The coincidence of the concern with circumcision in the Merina revolt and in early Christianity points to a much more fundamental similarity than the mere concern with cutting off the same bit of flesh. The early Christians, like the Merina, were disillusioned with their politico-religious leadership, which they felt had abandoned them and their transcendental righteousness, and in order to renew the order of symbolical reproduction they re-emphasised the religious sequence of rebounding conquest by, in the one case, uniting symbolically with their ancestors and, in the other, with their God. In both cases, however, having given up hope of a mundane solution to their ills, they refused the re-entry implied by the second conquest of alien and conquered vitality. And so they attempted to remain beyond life as ancestors or to join the crucified Christ. In this way, the centrality of the notion of a welcomed death in both systems is readily comprehensible. Both systems accepted the first conquest, both were longing to escape entrapment in an unsatisfactory existence by moving towards the death of their own vitality in the way we have already seen in Buid mediumship, Shona spirit possession, Japanese Buddhism and Ladakhi marriage. But unlike all these other cases, the first Christians and the Merina of 1863 refused to replace their lost internal vitality by consumed vitality.

Things are not quite so simple, however. Interestingly, the Christian example shows another similarity with the Merina case and that is typically a somewhat ambivalent attitude towards such an absolute solution. As far as we can know from the fragmentary evidence of his epistles it seems as if Paul was either hedging his bets or, rather, that he was unsure what was going to happen. He seems to have been hesitating between, on the one hand, the millenarian alternative which completely turns its back on reproduction in the wide sense of the word and which therefore seems to be the preparation of a world-wide funeral and, on the other hand, prudent organisation of a well-organised church firmly embedded in the continuing practical and political world. One does not need to credit Paul with foreknowledge of the future to deduce from certain passages in the epistles that from very early on he was considering the possibility of linking up the nascent Christian churches with an earthly state, either a state centred on Jerusalem or possibly with Rome. Paul was after all proud of his Roman citizenship and seems to have been particularly anxious to maintain the authority of Rome. It is no accident that all his journeys were westward and that they ultimately took him to the capital of the empire.

In fact, of course, this fusing of Christianity and the Roman empire was only to happen long after Paul's death and the destruction of Jerusalem, but the possibility of some political base for Christianity seems to have been envisaged fairly early on. This possibility, and its eventual realisation, are reflected in Christian theology, in what is at least a change of emphasis. I noted above how Paul either did not hold a belief in the virgin birth or was so uninterested in the notion as not to mention it (Armstrong 1983: 128). Later in the history of Christianity, however, the belief in the virgin birth of Christ became a central dogma and was the subject of much controversy. This change is a significant aspect of the new political direction of later Christianity.

The concept of the virgin birth is something of a misnomer since the central idea that lies behind the doctrine is not about the absence of sexual intercourse but rather about the presence of Mary's intercourse with the divine.[4] It is an idea about mediation, the entry of a male divine into an earthly woman. As such, this idea refers to many themes which have been touched on in the earlier part of this book. Sexual and marital relations are often merged with ideas about the conquest of vitality by a transcendental subject for its own purposes. Thus, if Christian theology was the imitation of Christ and if Paul was asking Christians to die with Christ and become transcendental themselves, the virgin birth was the invitation to celebrate the re-entry of the divine into the vital through the sexual conquest of a woman, a conquest which must have involved all the overtones of violence which sex and marriage have always carried in Mediterranean cultures. Although, unlike some of our other examples, the believers probably identified in this case less with the penetrator than the penetrated the basic pattern remains the same. In other words the idea of the virgin birth was one of the ways in which the image of the second conquest of rebounding violence was reintroduced, an image which had originally been abandoned in the more millenarian phase of very early Christianity.

The image of the virgin birth thus took on the symbolic place vacated by the abandonment of the centrality of Jewish obedience to the law of Moses and of circumcision in the period when millenarianism stopped being dominant in Christianity. The idea of the virgin birth then became particularly suitable to a church which saw itself, like Mary, as the continuing earthly vessel of the divine, 'the bride of Christ'.

But, of course, it was not just the church which was penetrated by Christ in the symbolism of the virgin birth, but society or rather the polity, in this case the Roman empire (Leach 1983, chapter 4). Once again an image could be evoked of a communal body which, because it had submitted to Christ and willingly surrendered its vitality with Him, could legitimately recover vitality through rebounding violence. In this way Christianity, which had begun by a refusal of the continuation of earthly authority and conquest, could become like ancient Judaism, an ideology by which states and individuals could legitimate aggression and conquest.

This view of Christianity as involving an element of aggressive reconquest of the vitality of outside beings may seem somewhat alien to some modern Christians and there is no doubt that the earlier millenarian aspect of the religion never completely disappeared. However, the aggressive ideology of rebounding conquest has also been very evident in Christianity, as in other systems. This element was particularly evident during the crusades or when religious fervour could be backed by military might, as in the periods of European colonial expansion.

Of course, all this was to happen much later than the time of the epistles, but there is already a fundamental uncertainty in the epistles between millenarianism, which involves stopping at the first conquest, and joining in the rebound. On the whole the epistles opt for the former possibility. Later, the uncertainty remained, but most of the time it was the full model of rebounding violence which was to come to dominate, at least in high places.

This indeterminacy is not, however, unique to European Christianity, but occurs to a varying extent in all millenarian movements. For example, it recurs in a Christian context in the millenarian movements of the nineteenth- and twentieth-century Philippines which have been studied in Ileto's book *Pasyon and Revolution* (1979). In these movements Philippine rebels adopted the symbolism of the death and crucifixion of Christ to justify suicidal attacks on the powers of the moment in an attempt to end it all and bring about a transcendental millennial order which would exist on the other side of death. This symbolism only emerges strongly, however, when the attempt at political revolt is failing. When there is still hope to establish a more practical order the orthodox stress on mediation reappears, though often in very unorthodox forms. This hesitation is characteristic of all such movements and, indeed, it was also characteristic of the Merina revolt discussed above. Some people at certain moments were tipping towards bringing back the rule of the ancestors once and for all, while others at various moments during the insurrection seemed to favour a new mediation involving the second act of conquest in rebounding violence which would have occurred with the completion of the circumcision ritual. Thus, some of the rebels of 1863 wanted actually to carry out the circumcision ceremony to the full, go to the ancestors through possession but also come back and consume women and plants and thereby regain vitality. This reinstitution of the second conquest, however, was only achieved by the government which took over after the murder of Radama II, when for a while the old order was re-established and the royal circumcision ritual carried out once more.

But, in fact, this hesitancy is not limited to such dramatic millenarian outbreaks, which are typical of extreme historical circumstances. It occurs in more or less muted form in all the rituals I have discussed, where the sequence of rebounding conquest always suggests the possibility of refusing the return. In every ritual one feels that people are contemplating the possibility of absolute transcendence and are more or less enthusiastic about the violent return. Thus we saw how in Orokaiva initiation the idea that the initiates may never come back from seclusion is a major theme of the discourse *about* the ritual and Shona history gives us examples of similar movements to the Merina revolt of 1863 when people considered the possibility of abandoning all earthly rulers and simply joining the ancestors on the other side of death.

The presence of the millennial possibility of refusing the completion of rebounding violence in systems which celebrate it centrally takes a number of forms which are present in some of the examples discussed in the earlier chapters but which so far have not been touched on.

Thus, in the discussion of Dinka sacrifice, I concerned myself only with those sacrifices which end in the ceremonial feast at which the victim is eaten. There are, however, also much less common sacrifices when the flesh of the victim is abandoned. These tend to occur when it is felt that something truly awful has happened, for example a particularly bad case of incest. In these cases it is as if the only solution, for a while at least, is to leave vitality altogether and not return to the scene of the disaster and so the sacrificer does not consume the meat.

An even clearer example of the presence of the millenarian possibility in non-millenarian circumstances is offered by the existence of certain individuals who have taken this tack in a world intent on the second conquest. The Buddhist monks of Japan would be an example of such people and so would Hindu ascetics. Thus Parry, in his study of Benares, tells us of the necrophagous ascetics who haunt the funeral grounds (Parry 1982). These are people who demonstrate by their outrageous behaviour that they are not any more of this world and are therefore free of its conventions. Their initiation into asceticism has been a form of funeral which did not involve the cosmogonic fire of sacrifice. They have accepted, therefore, the surrender of their vitality implied by the first part of rebounding conquest but not the second. They are, therefore, like the Merina rebels or like the millenarian Christians but living in a society which is centrally governed by the full sequence.

Thus, the element of doubt and uncertainty is as important in the ethnography of the systems I have examined as the apparently over-certain sequences which, for the sake of presentation, I have previously emphasised. Indeed, it is this element of doubt which explains the indirect relation of the political situation to ritual symbolism and individual experience.

The symbolism of rebounding violence offers at least three alternative avenues of legitimate practice and in addition any mixture of the three: (1) the assertion of reproduction; (2) the legitimation of expansionism, which itself takes one of two forms: (a) it may be internally directed, in which case it legitimates social hierarchy or (b) it may be externally directed and become an encouragement to aggression against neighbours; (3) the abandonment of earthly existence. In any particular instance or historical moment one of the alternatives will dominate but the others will also be present in more or less shadowy forms. Which particular alternative dominates and informs action is largely, though not exclusively, determined by people's evaluation of their politico-economic circumstances, whether they are likely to be able to defeat their neighbours, whether they can succeed in maintaining themselves or whether the situation is so hopeless that they abandon reproduction.

It is because the symbolism of rebounding violence, which at bottom is concerned with the universal social, political, intellectual and emotional problem of human fluidity, can be used for such a wide variety of political circumstances and to legitimate such apparently opposed practices that the same idiom can survive and adapt to so many contexts.

7

Myth

Chapter 6 consisted of a discussion of the way in which it is possible to reverse the predatory implications of rebounding violence by arresting the progression half-way, at the point when native vitality has been abandoned but before restrengthening external vitality has been consumed. This possibility comes to the fore when political circumstances make all forms of social continuation appear hopeless. In many ways this millenarian transformation can be thought of as revolutionary in that it may lead to political upheaval, as it did in Madagascar in 1863. However, in spite of this political radicalism, there is a sense in which the millenarian option is also intellectually conservative. It does not reject the symbolism of conquest in rebounding violence; it merely seeks to abort the sequence. To find a truly radical challenge occurring on a sufficiently regular basis as to be recorded by ethnographers, it is necessary to leave the realm of organised practice for the most part and move to the freer speculation of what has been called myth.[1] It is, however, quite possible that such speculation may hover in the background and occur quite frequently in the minds of the peoples we have so far discussed, but, nonetheless, only rarely achieve the public formulation which would make the recording of this type of thinking likely.

This chapter deals with such radical rejections, but since these occur in the world of imagination, it leads the argument away from the main concern of the book, which is actual practice and the linked experiences it evokes. This final part of the book is therefore perhaps best seen as a sort of appendix, or as a sketchy joint speculation by the author and the subjects of the ethnographies discussed concerning how matters might be if everything was different and the attempt to establish transcendental institutions had not even been attempted.

There was a time when anthropologists saw a direct relation between myth and practice, for example Malinowski (1948) and also Leach (1954). However, Lévi-Strauss has shown quite conclusively how misleading such an approach actually is (1958, chapter 11). He has pointed out how mythology is so often a speculation on practice, exploring all imaginable possibilities in what must remain an intellectual search. Myths often seem simply to review the possible doubts of the participants and explore these with horrified fascination. Myths seem to concentrate on the terrifying or ironic possibilities of the failure of the system (Huntington 1988: 79) or on the impossibility of its teleological implications rather than, as anthropologists used to believe, provide a charter for action.

From what I know of mythology in different parts of the world such a view seems largely correct and it is unfortunate that the radical difference between the general discourse of mythology and most forms of ritual practice is so often forgotten by anthropologists whose study implicitly homologises the two different types of data. However, Lévi-Strauss's view also requires a certain amount of qualification. The distinction between myth and ritual is not quite as sharp as he makes out, nor does it correspond exactly with the dividing line between the two phenomena as they are usually understood. (Lévi-Strauss 1971: 596–603). In the example of the Ma'Betisek to be discussed below we find that the kind of radical intellectual adventurousness and refusal of distinction which Lévi-Strauss identifies with myth sometimes also spills over into ritual practice. Secondly, we find that there are some myths which do indeed serve as charters for conservative social practices and for rituals which construct rebounding violence.

The anthropologist with experience of fieldwork will also be well aware that even the most speculative myths are not quite the relaxed, curious speculation which Lévi-Strauss seems to suggest. When we look at mythology in context we get the feeling that the intellectual is much more driven, much more anxious and more directed than we would imagine from reading his work. In particular, myths are so often directed to a painful consideration of the problems hidden by the treacherously easy solutions which the rituals of rebounding violence propose.

We have already come across a number of myths and practices in this book which can serve to make these points. In chapter 5 it was pointed out that the combination of self-denial and aggression present in Ladakhi marriage was often related to a myth which among other things illustrates bride capture. This is the story of the mythical king and hero Kesar who, after many adventures, regains his bride and lives happily ever after. These final episodes are the events which the rituals of marriage are seen to evoke, but in fact this part of the story is only a little section of the total myth, in which we find that before settling the matter quite so satisfactorily Kesar had a much more uncertain marital career.

In the full story Kesar, himself the product of bizarre unions, first marries a princess by stealth and becomes incorporated into her father's kingdom in contradiction of the rule of virilocality. He next kills an ogre and goes on to live with the ogre's wife and produce a child. Meanwhile, his former wife moves in with a new husband. Finally, after much complication Kesar abandons his second wife and recaptures the first. Such bewildering accounts of behaviour which goes against the morality thought appropriate for more ordinary mortals are in fact typical of myths which Malinowski so misleading considered as 'charters' for social institutions. Although one cannot rule out the possibility that they might well be that, they are therefore also much else besides.

In her careful study of this myth Phylactou shows how the different stages of the story evoke many of the possibilities of marriage permutations that can be envisaged within the Tibetan cultural framework. Not only do we have a story which corresponds fairly closely to an ideal marriage, where the bride is triumphantly taken back to the groom's house, but we also have the opposite, where the groom is incorporated into his wife's house, and also many other variants on the general theme of marriage.

The fact that the Kesar myth dwells on the possibility of the hero's being absorbed in his wife's family is typical of myth. We find again and again in myth the imaginary consideration of worlds without rebounding violence or of worlds where the consumed become the consumers. Thus in Orokaiva mythology we find stories of pigs which, because they have been captured and penetrated by ancestral spirits, can therefore, like initiated humans, hunt, capture and eat both pigs and humans. Such evocations are thus radical fantasies, imagining what would happen if the sequence of rebounding violence was reversed so that it ended with the consumption of humans by pigs. Referring to an analogous myth, Iteanu is thus able to say that: 'In the myth initiation is represented as the negative of what it is in the ritual' (Iteanu 1983: 71).

Again, if we turn to Buid ethnography we find similar ideas. The Buid see their relation to predatory spirits, which are themselves sometimes imagined as giant pigs, as pig-like (Gibson 1986: 154). That is, in the images of myth and in the visions of spirit mediums, the horrifying possibility of being consumed by those beings they consume emerges in Buid imagination. In such images we have a truly radical potential challenge to the order established by rebounding violence, even if it remains almost exclusively in the realm of the imaginary.

In order to illustrate such subversive thought I conclude this book with one more example from a stimulating ethnography by Wazir-Jahan Karim of a South East Asian people, the Ma'Betisek (Karim 1981). The Ma'Betisek are an aboriginal group from Malaysia who now live in very precarious conditions, powerless, driven from their land and surrounded by much more powerful neighbours. Karim identifies as the root of Ma'Betisek religious ideas two fundamental and largely incompatible principles, which she denotes by the Ma'Betisek uses of the words *tulah* and *kemali'*. *Tulah* can be translated into English as either 'domination' or 'curse'. The two meanings are linked in that legitimate domination is the result of a successful curse. Thus, if a member of a senior generation feels he has in some way been slighted by a junior, he may curse him. The junior will then, as a result of the curse, lose his rights as a human being. If we envisage this form of cursing within the schema of rebounding violence it means that, if a junior refuses to be conquered by his senior, he then loses his right to conquer in turn and thus becomes like a plant or an animal who can be consumed with impunity.

One aspect of the curse of *tulah* which particularly interests Karim and the Ma'Betisek is its significance for defining the food one may eat. Like many Asian and Amerindian peoples the Ma'Betisek consider plants, animals and humans as having been originally so closely linked as to have been almost identical. Thus plants and animals are sometimes seen as descended from humans who, because of overcrowding in villages which existed in the distant past, had to move out to the forest. Sometimes, in a somewhat similar way, plants and animals are believed to have originated from the souls of dead humans (Karim 1981: 45, 67).

In the past therefore plants, animals and humans were continually interacting in a somewhat promiscuous fashion. However, in the end, plants and animals seem to have failed to observe the fundamental rules of mutual co-operation and sharing which common residence should imply and instead they were found to be doing the very opposite. They were secretly killing and eating humans, thereby being guilty of eating their own kind, i.e. cannibalism, since at that time all living forms were undifferentiated and therefore one (Karim 1981: 34). Because of this immoral behaviour towards those one should co-operate with, the elders cursed the plants and animals with the curse of *tulah*. This meant that from then on plants and animals could be exploited and eaten by humans. From having been illegitimate killers and hunters, plants and animals became legitimate prey. Humans, for their part, were henceforth able to kill and consume plants and animals legitimately. Because they had once been food, humans could be eaters: they had changed from prey into hunters. This story, therefore, explains why, for the Ma'Betisek, plants and animals can be consumed by humans and why plants and animals cannot consume humans in return.

As it stands the story follows the pattern of rebounding violence perfectly. Humans, plants and animals share a lot, but are also distinguished by the presence or absence of one critical element, which is rather like the spirit element of the Orokaiva, or the speech element of the Dinka. What makes humans more than plants and animals is that they obey the social rules enforced by elders, especially those prototypical social rules forbidding cannibalism and incest. Because they obey and submit to the transcendental element implied in following these rules, in other words because they allow their native vitality to be regulated, the Ma'Betisek obtain, according to the logic of rebounding violence, the right to consume the vitality, by now external and alien, of those beings which had refused the first conquest. The plants and animals by their failure have become *other* forms of living things who henceforth have to live in *other* places and humans can therefore legitimately feed on them.

But even within this confident formulation of the legitimation of consumption the shadow of doubt is not far away. After all, by explaining why they may consume other living things the Ma'Betisek are also acknowledging the potentially dismaying fact of the initial identity of all forms of life. This inevitably raises the suggestion of questions such as what, for example, would have happened if the plants and animals had not been cursed? Then the hunting, killing and consumption of plants and animals would be both illegitimate and horrifying. It would be a form of cannibalism, the very crime which would justify plants and animals consuming humans.

This possibility seems to be continually envisaged in such cultures as a haunting undeveloped theme in the orchestration of meaning. To keep such eventualities from becoming realities, the Ma'Betisek, like many other South East Asian peoples, seem obsessive about maintaining boundaries between humans and other life forms, by, for example, insisting on the contrast between the raw food of plants and animals and the cooked food of humans and by expressing the fear that any act of over-familiarity on the part of humans towards animals or plants will bring about a cosmic calamity (Needham 1964). However, it is when things go wrong and illness strikes that the fear of the possibility of the reversal of rebounding violence, caused by the near-cannibalism implied in eating plants and animals, really comes to the fore. This is shown by the fact that the Ma'Betisek attribute the cause of all the most serious diseases to a kind of revenge on the part of the plants and animals against the humans. This retaliation is envisaged as taking the form of diseases which result from the attacks of animal and plant spirits avenging themselves for the illegitimate consumption of their species.

In a manner that is similar to the African curers discussed in chapter 3, the Ma'Betisek deal with such problems of invasion in one of two ways. The first is akin to the first tack of African diviners, that is, they attempt to expel the invading animal or plant spirit. As noted above, among the Ma'Betisek trouble is attributed to the idea that the curse enacted so long ago, which made plants and animals the legitimate prey of humans, does not hold any more and so the plants and animals have been able to take their revenge. If the curse is weak this means that the differentiation between humans, on the one hand, and plants and animals, on the other, has been breached and so eating plants and animals has become once more cannibalism and is therefore punishable. The image of this state of affairs is all the more horrific as an idea because the original reason for the *tulah* curse which made them eatable was precisely that it was a punishment administered to plants and animals because of their cannibalism. But now, if the curse is not holding, it is the humans who are the cannibals and it would therefore follow that plants and animals would be justified in their spirit attacks on people.

The first Ma'Betisek solution to such a state of affairs is to restore the *status quo* and to drive out the plant and animal spirits yet again, by re-enacting the original curse against them and thereby re-establishing the legitimacy of human consumption. The curse used by qualified elders on such an occasion could not express more clearly the idea that the problem is that the original separation of plants and animals and humans is no longer as clear as it should be and that it must, therefore, be re-established: 'if an animal, *be* an animal; if human, *be* a human; but do not be both human and animal' (Karim 1981: 39, italics added).

This first tack, however, may not always be fully satisfactory, as is shown when the disease persists. Then the Ma'Betisek try a second tack. This is, however, quite unlike the second tack of people like the Dinka who, as we saw, simply re-enact the process of rebounding violence with still greater emphasis through sacrifice. What the Ma'Betisek do on such occasions actually implies the total abandonment of the symbolism of rebounding violence and at the same time the whole attempt to establish a life-transcending social order which differentiates people from other life forms. In a way which must have much to do with their political powerlessness they refuse the whole system on which human societies build their claim to transcendence and thereby conjure up a truly radical rejection of rebounding violence in ritual. They do this by abandoning the principle of *tulah* and by turning instead to their second religious idea, that of *kemali'*.

Kemali' thought occurs much less frequently in practical and political circumstances than does *tulah* thought. As Lévi-Stauss would have predicted, it comes to the fore in certain types of myth which stress the indistinguishable aspects of all living things. *Kemali'* thought emphasises the continuity between plants, humans and animals, which are all seen as mutually helpful siblings. In this perspective every act of consumption is an illegitimate act of aggression and the fragile basis of *tulah* is negated. By stressing unity *kemali'* myth inevitably raises the disturbing questions: What if plants and animals were truly our sisters and brothers? What if the extra transcendental element which distinguishes humans from other life forms was a mere illusion?

This doubt, as we have seen, is the source of Ma'Betisek explanations of disease and can sometimes be dealt with by a re-emphasis of *tulah*; however, *kemali'* ideas can also be used for curing. This occurs in shamanistic sessions when, with the help of animal and plant spirit familiars, a kind of temporary peace and community among all living forms is evoked through dance, song and the sharing of food which is half raw, half cooked, thereby symbolising the lack of differentiation between humans and animals (1981: 195). It is as if the state of existence in myth as it was before the curse of *tulah* was being reinstated in the present and human beings had abdicated their superiority. This tack brings about respite from disease because, once the siblingship of all species has been established, there is no room for anybody consuming anybody else and it would therefore be unreasonable for the plant and animal spirits to continue their interference with humans.

This solution is achieved, however, at a very great cost. It implies the abandonment of the claim to the superiority of human society; it implies the abandonment of the attempt to transcend process by establishing permanent structures; it implies the abandonment of all forms of consumption. This is the most radical solution of all, though obviously one which cannot be maintained for long. Unlike millenarianism it does not just refuse the second half of rebounding violence, but rejects the whole process. It is a solution which implies a practice that has learnt the implicit lesson of the critical commentary on human existence found in myth, which asks, rather like an anarchist critique of society, what if the consumers were the consumed? But even for such an unassuming group of people as the Ma'Betisek such liberating humility can only be a temporary solution. After all one must eat. The seance finished, the world of *tulah* must be discreetly re-established so that food can once more be obtained, so that society can continue and so that the world of rebounding violence may regain its full potential for conquest of other species and of oneself.

To end here is perhaps to suggest that, given the raw materials of our shared perceptions of the processes of life and with the limited tools of ritualisation and metaphor at our disposal, the constructions of rebounding violence, in their many structural forms and contents, are the only way in which the necessary image of society as a transcendental and legitimate order can be constructed. This would also mean, therefore, that we cannot construct cosmologies other than those which offer a toe-hold to the legitimation of domination and violence. But perhaps the Ma'Betisek example shows something quite different. It may show that, when in real trouble, we are able to analyse and criticise the very basis of our ideologies, to begin to demystify ourselves and to search for fundamentally different solutions.

Notes

2 Initiation

1. For some reason Iteanu (1983) translates this shout as 'Bite, kill, bite' although his sources Williams and Chinnery and Beaver translate the words as I have done.
2. Chinnery and Beaver 1915: 77, quoted in Iteanu 1983.
3. This part of the proceedings might well be called a pig corrida, not only because of the ritualised chase but also because of the treatment of partly domesticated animals as though they were wild ones. This has been argued by Pitt-Rivers (1983). In fact the whole matter is more complicated in that the way the Orokaiva deal with their pigs means that even domesticated pigs appear as though they were captured from the wild state.
4. All pigs are born wild in the bush and they have to be captured both symbolically and literally to become domesticated and like human children. This is like what happens to human children both at initiation and immediately after birth. After birth children go through a ritual which seems to represent them as at first analogous to plants. They then have to be conquered as plants to become like pigs. This first ritual is therefore like what happens to domesticated pigs when they are captured from the bush. However, humans will then go on to repeat the process at initiation while pigs will not. It is therefore important to remember that the process of transformation of prey into hunter has already occurred once before initiation for Orokaiva children in that they have been symbolically changed immediately after birth by conquest from taro into pigs and that pigs are the hunters of taro (see Iteanu 1983, chapter 1).
5. I find it interesting to speculate on the possibility that the well-known theory put forward by Rappaport (1984 (1968)) concerning the ecological competition between pigs and humans among the Maring may owe a lot to the actors' own symbolism concerned with the similarities and differences of pigs and humans.
6. This point is particularly well made by Hirsch for another nearby New Guinea people (Hirsch 1987). Similarly L. Josephides notes how among the Kewa a pig's cry is often said to resemble a child's (personal communication).
7. Of course there is a problem here in that in many languages the word for owner and parent is the same but I feel it is clear from the other evidence that we are genuinely dealing with notions of parenthood here.
8. Photo in Iteanu 1983, p. 41.
9. The Orokaiva believe that sometimes pigs are conquered by spirits; when this

happens the pigs become like a superior enemy which will kill humans instead of the humans killing the pigs.

10. Among the nearby Fuyuge the hunter calls out the name of the surrounding mountains where the spirits live at that moment (Hirsch, personal communication).

11. This seems very common throughout New Guinea: see Strathern 1985 and Hirsch 1987. It seems to me likely that the 'catherine wheel' performed by the 'spirits' imitates the birds of paradise.

12. The relationship to a spirit of the dead, usually a grandparent, is first established at the original child-planting ceremony (see above, n. 4).

13. In using the word hierarchical I am following Iteanu's (1983) analysis because I feel his stress on this aspect is illuminating. However, unlike Iteanu, I am not satisfied to leave the matter at simply an observation on the formal aspects of the symbolism.

14. Schwimmer (1973: 138) notes the physiological effect of meat eating on people with a diet such as that of the Orokaiva.

15. Of course, as noted above, this combination is again expressed when the hunter is about to kill a pig and when he momentarily identifies himself with a spirit.

16. Hirsch, personal communication.

17. For example, in the initiation hut the old live above the young, a straightforward reversal of the normal situation.

3 Sacrifice

1. All quotations from the Bible in this book are taken from *The Jerusalem Bible*.

2. This criticism of course also applies to the subsequent book by Durkheim: *Les Formes élémentaires de la vie religieuse* 1912, which seems to follow in part from Hubert and Mauss's essay on sacrifice.

3. It is interesting to note in this respect that the clan divinity of the masters of the fishing spear is Flesh. At first sight this might seem contrary to what we might expect until we are told that the flesh associated with this divinity is precisely the twitching flesh which marks the final victory of speech.

4. Gibson makes it clear that pigs have souls and this explains the possibility of their becoming spirits after death, but I am less certain that for the Buid all animals have souls.

5. One manifestation of this is the taboo on laughing at copulating animals, which would somehow endanger this boundary.

6. Gibson rules out the possibility that the pig is given as a substitute on the basis of the fact that none of the meat is given to the spirits. This is unconvincing. In his discussion of other Buid sacrifice Gibson has no problem in saying that the pig is given to the spirits even though they hardly get any meat. Thus in his discussion of sacrifice to the *Afu Daga* he says 'it is the life of the pig ... which is being offered' (1986: 175). The reason why no meat at all is given in this case is made clear by Gibson when he points out that in sacrifice to evil spirits, unlike other sacrifices, there is no question of inviting the spirits to share in the human feast-giving. In any case, such reasoning would rule out a similar explanation in very many cases where, as here, no meat is given to the supernatural being, although the fact that the victim is given as a substitute is made quite explicit. An example of this would be ancient Greek sacrifice discussed above. The alternative explanation given by Gibson concerns the nature of animal and spatial symbolism among the Buid. This

discussion is to me quite convincing but does not explain why the ritual should drive away the evil spirits.

7. In his enthusiasm to disagree with Evans-Pritchard and Lienhardt he goes so far as to say 'the notion that human life and animal life may be regarded as somehow equivalent is at complete variance with Buid ideas concerning the cosmic hierarchy of predator and prey' (p. 179) but his discussion on animal classification implies, as noted above, quite strong ideas of substitutability, pp. 152–8.

4 Cosmogony and the state

1. I am assuming, following Heesterman (1985, *passim*) that, in terms of the wider symbolism, the ascetic and the Brahman are extremely close.

2. The royal symbolism of cremation is supported by the fact that theoretically only Rajas and Maharajas should be cremated on the very spot of Vishnu's cosmogony (Parry, personal communication).

3. In this brief discussion I ignore the new religions of Japan as well as Christianity though I believe that to include them would not contradict the general conclusions outlined here.

4. These dogs were originally lions (S. Tanabe, personal communication).

5. This is the western paradise of orthodox Buddhism but it appears that as far as ordinary people are concerned the idea of paradise remains totally vague and not unlike similar concepts in Christianity.

6. These are called in Japanese *Butsu-Stan* meaning Buddhist altar and the phrase is normally translated into English as Buddhist shrine. In this book, however, I shall call them miniature 'temples', partly to underline their similarity with the larger temples and also to distinguish them from Shinto shrines.

7. For example the food is carried behind people's backs so that the ancestors will not catch the eye of the living and thereby gather what is happening.

8. For fuller descriptions of the rituals involved the reader should refer to the encyclopedic *Ancestor Worship in Contemporary Japan* by R. J. Smith 1974. This book contains a wealth of further references.

9. Of course during the period between the Meiji restoration until the American administration after the war Shinto became organised as a national institution centred ever more on the Emperor, and something of this remains now.

10. It is highly significant that Shinto priests use salt for purification since in many rituals salt marks separation from the dead. For example, when leaving a cemetery people sprinkle salt behind themselves.

11. It is true that during the period when there was an attempt to build up Shintoism into an organised state religion, Shinto funeral rites were invented and these sometimes can still be found. However, for most people most of the time Shinto cannot cope with deaths other than those of the Emperors or the war dead, which somehow avoid pollution.

12. In some exceptional cases, as in Kyoto, these final rituals also have a Buddhist element. This is because of the historical association of the city. However, even here the Shinto elements are also strong and the general character of the ritual is typical of what Japanese associate with Shintoism.

13. The contrast between the varnished and lacquered objects of Buddhism and the unglazed and unvarnished objects of Shintoism is a powerful symbolic theme which in part expresses the ideas of purity and 'primitivism' characteristic of Shintoism.

14. Of course a certain amount of caution needs be exercised in this identification of the gods of Shintoism with the ancestors of Buddhism since those Japanese who argued this were doing so as part of building up the nationalist idiom, which dominated until the end of the war. However, the fact that such a construction was possible indicates that the idea was already present.

5 Marriage

1. It is interesting to note that the genitalia are then eaten by the women led by the senior wives. It would appear that this eating of masculinity by the female affine of the sacrificing lineage underlies the sexual idiom of the second part of the sacrificing by inverting it (Lienhardt 1961: 269).
2. In fact the ritual anticipates the true rebounding conquest which will occur when the penetrated household will itself become the invader as it takes wives from another household. This occurs at the moment when the bride leaves her natal house, a departure which, as we have seen, has associations with the loss of its grain store. At that moment, as if to compensate for the loss, the natal household of the bride celebrates a mock harvest festival as if in anticipation of the harvest which will follow the loss.
3. In Tibet the opposition between the male stuff and the female element is in terms of the opposition between bone and blood.
4. A similar point is made by Leach in *Political Systems of Highland Burma* (Leach 1954, chapter 7).

6 Millenarianism

1. It seems that, for the Merina, women are thought to become ancestors more slowly than men.
2. Bateson uses the word much more widely but on page 178 he uses it in exactly the way intended here in relation to what is also an initiation ritual (Bateson 1958).
3. All biblical quotations are from *The Jerusalem Bible*.
4. Much of the discussion of this topic in anthropology and elsewhere seems to me totally unsatisfactory because it forgets this simple point (Leach 1967).

7 Myth

1. There are in fact a whole range of types of linguistic behaviours which have been labelled myth by anthropologists and they have very different sociological implications. Not since Malinowski has a serious attempt been made to try to classify them. It is clearly inappropriate for me to try to do so here and in this discussion I am merely using the word loosely, much in the way it has been used by Lévi-Strauss.

References

Armstrong, K. 1983. *The First Christians: St. Paul's Impact on Christianity*. London: Pan.

Atran, S. 1987. 'Ordinary constraints on the semantics of living kinds: a commonsense alternative to recent treatment of natural object terms'. *Mind and Language* 2: 27–68.

Bateson, G. 1958. (second edition) *Naven*. Stanford: Stanford University Press.

Beidelman, T. O. 1966. 'Swazi royal ritual'. *Africa* 36: 373–405.

Biardeau, M. 1972. *Clefs pour la pensée Hindoue*. Paris: Seghers.

Biardeau, M. and C. Malamoud 1976. *Le Sacrifice dans l'Inde ancienne*. Paris: P.U.F.

Bloch, M. 1974. 'Symbol, song and dance and features of articulation: or is religion an extreme form of traditional authority?' *Archives Européennes de Sociologie* 15: 55–81.

1985. 'From cognition to ideology' in R. Fardon (ed.) *Power and Knowledge: Anthropological and Sociological Approaches*. Edinburgh: Scottish University Press.

1986. *From Blessing to Violence: History and Ideology in the Circumcision Ritual of the Merina of Madagascar*. Cambridge: Cambridge University Press.

1988. 'Death and the concept of the person' in S. Cederroth, C. Corlin and J. Lindstrom (eds.) *On the Meaning of Death*. Uppsala: Acta Universitatis Upsaliensis.

Burkert, W. 1983. *Homo Necans: The Anthropology of Ancient Greek Sacrificial Ritual and Myth*, translated by P. Bing. Berkeley: University of California Press.

Burling, R. 1963. *Rengsanggri: Family and Kinship in a Garo Village*. Philadelphia: University of Philadelphia Press.

Burridge, K. 1969. *New Heaven, New Earth*. Oxford: Blackwell.

Cassirer, E. 1972. *Philosophies des formes symboliques*. Paris: Gallimard.

Chinnery, E. W. P. and W. N. Beaver 1915. 'Notes on the initiation ceremonies of the Koko, Papua'. *Journal of the Royal Anthropological Institute* 45: 69–78.

Cohn, N. 1957. *The Pursuit of the Millennium*. London: Secker and Warburg.

Dale Saunders, E. 1964. *Buddhism in Japan*. Tokyo: Tuttle.

Day, S. 1989. 'Embodying spirits: village oracles and possession ritual in Ladakh, North India'. Ph.D thesis, University of London.

Detienne, M. 1979. 'Pratiques culinaires et esprit de sacrifice' in J.-P. Vernant and M. Detienne (eds.) *La Cuisine du sacrifice en pays grec*. Paris: Gallimard.

Dumont, L. 1977. *Homo Aequalis: Genèse et épanouissement de l'idéologie économique.* Paris: Gallimard.

Durkheim, E. 1912. *Les Formes élémentaires de la vie religieuse.* Paris: Alcan.

Eliade, M. 1969. *Le Mythe de l'éternel retour.* Paris: Gallimard.

Embree, J. F. 1939. *Suye Mura: A Japanese Village.* Chicago: University of Chicago Press.

Evans-Pritchard, E. E. 1956. *Nuer Religion.* Oxford: Oxford University Press.

Fortes, M. 1953. 'The structure of unilineal descent groups'. *American Anthropologist* 55: 17–41.

Friedman, J. and M. Rowlands 1977. 'Notes toward an epigenetic model of the evolution of civilization' in J. Friedman and M. Rowlands (eds.) *The Evolution of Social Systems.* London: Duckworth.

Fuller, C. 1984. *Servants of the Goddess: The Priests of a South Indian Temple.* Cambridge: Cambridge University Press.

Gibson, T. 1986. *Sacrifice and Sharing in the Philippine Highlands.* London School of Economics Monographs in Social Anthropology n.57. London: Athlone.

Gillison, G. 1980. 'Images of nature in Gimi thought' in C. MacCormack and M. Strathern (eds.) *Nature, Culture and Gender.* Cambridge: Cambridge University Press.

Girard, R. 1972. *La Violence et le sacré.* Paris: Gallimard.

Gough, K. 1955. 'Female initiation cults of the Malabar coast'. *Journal of the Royal Anthropological Institute* 85: 458.

1969. 'The Nayars and the definition of marriage'. *Journal of the Royal Anthropological Institute* 89: 23–34.

Headley, S. (ed.) 1987. *De la hutte au palais.* Paris: C.N.R.S.

Heesterman, J. C. 1985. *The Inner Conflict of Tradition: Essays in Indian Ritual, Kingship and Society.* Chicago: University of Chicago Press.

de Heusch, L. 1986. *Le Sacrifice dans les religions africaines.* Paris: Gallimard.

Hirsch, E. 1987. 'Dialects of the bower bird; an interpretive account of ritual and symbolism in the Udabe valley, Papua New Guinea'. *Mankind* 17: 1–14.

Hori, I. 1974. (originally published 1968) *Folk Religion in Japan: Continuity and Change.* Chicago: University of Chicago Press.

Hubert, H. and M. Mauss. 1968. 'Essai sur la nature et la fonction du sacrifice' in M. Mauss *Oeuvres Vol. I.* Paris: Editions de Minuit.

Huntington, R. 1988. *Gender and Social Structure in Madagascar.* Bloomington: Indiana University Press.

Ileto, R. C. 1979. *Pasyon and Revolution.* Manila: Atheneo de Manila.

Iteanu, A. 1983. *La Ronde des échanges. De la circulation aux valeurs chez les Orokaiva.* Cambridge: Cambridge University Press.

Karim, W-J. 1981. *Ma'Betisek Concepts of Living Things.* London School of Economics Monographs in Social Anthropology 54. London: Athlone.

Kautsky, K. 1953. *Foundations of Christianity: A Study of Christian Origins.* New York: International Publishers Co.

Kuchler, S. 1985. 'Malangan, exchange and regional integration in northern New Ireland'. Ph.D. thesis, University of London.

Lambek, M. 1981. *Human Spirits: A Cultural Account of Trance in Mayotte.* Cambridge: Cambridge University Press.

Lan, D. 1985. *Guns and Rain: Guerrillas and Spirit Mediumship in Zimbabwe.* London: James Currey.

Lanternari, V. 1963. *The Religions of the Oppressed.* London: McGibbon and Key.

Leach, E. R. 1954. *Political Systems of Highland Burma*. London: Bell.
  1967. 'Virgin birth'. *Proceedings of the Royal Anthropological Institute* 1966: 39–49.
  1983. 'Melchidesech and the Emperor' in E. R. Leach and D. A. Aycock *Structuralist Interpretations of Biblical Myth*. Cambridge: Cambridge University Press (originally published in the *Proceedings of the Royal Anthropological Institute* for 1972).
Lévi-Strauss, C. 1958. *Anthropologie structurale*. Paris: Plon.
  1962. *Le Totémisme aujourd'hui*. Paris: Plon.
  1971. *L'Homme nu. Mythologiques* 4. Paris: Plon.
  1984. *Paroles données*. Paris: Plon.
Lewis, G. 1980. *Day of Shining Red: An Essay on Understanding Ritual*. Cambridge: Cambridge University Press.
Lienhardt, G. 1961. *Divinity and Experience: The Religion of the Dinka*. Oxford: Oxford University Press.
  1985. 'Self: public, private. Some African representations' in M. Carrithers, S. Collins and S. Lukes (eds.) *The Category of the Person: Anthropology, Philosophy, History*. Cambridge: Cambridge University Press.
MacCormack, C. and M. Strathern 1980. *Nature, Culture and Gender*. Cambridge: Cambridge University Press.
McLennan, J. 1865. *Primitive Marriage: An Inquiry into the Origin of the Form of Capture in Marriage Ceremonies*. Edinburgh: A. and C. Black.
Malinowski, B. 1948. *Magic, Science and Religion*. Glencoe: The Free Press.
Mauss, M. 1923/4. 'Essai sur le don: formes et raisons de l'échange dans les sociétés archaïques'. *L'Année Sociologique*, 2nd series.
Middleton, J. 1960. *Lugbara Religion Ritual and Authority among an East African People*. Oxford: Oxford University Press.
Modjeska, N. 1982. 'Production and inequality: perspectives from central New Guinea' in A. Strathern (ed.) *Inequality in the New Guinea Highlands*. Cambridge: Cambridge University Press.
Needham, R. 1964. 'Blood, thunder and the mockery of animals'. *Sociologus* (N.S.) 14: 136–49.
  1971. 'Remarks on the analysis of kinship and marriage' in R. Needham (ed.) *Rethinking Kinship and Marriage*. Association of Social Anthropologists Monograph 11. London: Tavistock.
O'Hanlon, M. 1983. 'Handsome is as handsome does: display and betrayal in Whagi'. *Oceania* 53: 317–33.
Ono, S. 1962. *Shinto: the Kami Way*. Tokyo: Tuttle.
Parry, J. 1981. 'Death and cosmogony in Kashi'. *Contributions to Indian Sociology* N.S. 15: 337–65.
  1982. 'Sacrificial death and the necrophageous ascetic' in M. Bloch and J. Parry (eds.) *Death and the Regeneration of Life*. Cambridge: Cambridge University Press.
  1985. 'Death and digestion: the symbolism of food and eating in North Indian mortuary rites'. *Man* N.S. 20: 612–30.
Phylactou, M. 1989. 'Household organisation and marriage in Ladakh'. Ph.D. thesis, University of London.
Pitt-Rivers, J. 1983. 'Le sacrifice du taureau' *Le Temps de la réfléxion* 1983: 281–97.
Rappaport, R. A. 1984. (new edition) *Pigs for the Ancestors: Ritual in the Ecology of a New Guinea People*. New Haven: Yale University Press.
Robertson-Smith, W. 1889. *Lectures on the Religion of the Semites*. Edinburgh: Black.

Rosaldo, M. 1980. *Knowledge and Passion: Ilongot Notions of Self and Social Life.* Cambridge: Cambridge University Press.

Rosaldo, R. 1980. *Ilongot Headhunting 1883–1974.* Stanford: Stanford University Press.

Schwimmer, E. 1973. *Exchange in the Social Structure of the Orokaiva. Traditional and Emergent Ideologies on the Northern District of Papua.* London: Hurst and Co.

Smith, R. J. 1974. *Ancestor Worship in Contemporary Japan.* Stanford. Stanford University Press.

1978. *Kurusu: The Price of Progress in a Japanese Village. 1951–1975.* Folkestone: Dawson.

1983. *Japanese Society.* Cambridge: Cambridge University Press.

Sperber, D. 1985. 'Anthropology and psychology: towards an epidemiology of representations'. *Man* N.S.: 20: 73–89.

Stanner, W. E. H. 1960. 'On Aboriginal religion: II Sacramentalism, rite and myth'. *Oceania* 30 no. 4: 245–78.

Strathern, A. 1985. 'A line of boys: Melpa dance as a symbol of maturation' in P. Spencer (ed.) *Society and the Dance.* Cambridge: Cambridge University Press.

Strathern, M. 1979. 'The self in self decoration'. *Oceania* 49: 241–57.

1988. *The Gender of the Gift: Problems with Women and Problems with Society in Melanesia.* Berkeley: University of California Press.

Tambiah, S. J. 1970. *Buddhism and the Spirit Cult in North East Thailand.* Cambridge: Cambridge University Press.

Turner, V. 1969. *The Ritual Process.* London: Routledge, Kegan and Paul.

Van Gennep, A. 1909. *Les Rites de passage.* Paris: Nourry.

Vernant, J.-P. 1979. 'A la table des hommes' in J.-P. Vernant and M. Detienne (eds.) *La Cuisine du sacrifice en pays grec.* Paris: Gallimard.

Williams, F. E. 1925. 'Plant emblems among the Orokaiva'. *Journal of the Royal Anthropological Institute* 55: 405–25.

1930. *Orokaiva Society.* Oxford: Oxford University Press.

Yanagita, K. 1946. *Senzo no Hanashi.* Tokyo: Chikuma Shobo.

Zeitlyn, S. J. 1986. 'Sacrifice and the sacred in a Hindu Tintha: the case of Pushkan India'. Ph.D. thesis, University of London.

Index

114